Primitive Money
of Africa

Tales & Details

James Zylstra

Primitive Money of Africa: Tales and Details

James Zylstra

Copyright © 2018

Contents

Foreword by Robert D. Leonard Jr.   vii

Introduction   1

Part I: Tales   5

1. Money Matters   7

2. Money Milieu   25

3. Money in the Market   45

4. Money and Marriage   61

5. Money and the Merchants   81

6. Money and Metallurgy   99

7. Money Models   109

8. Money and Mystique   127

9. Money and Might   137

10. Money and Mourning   153

11. Money and Monetization   165

Part II: Details   181

1. Data, Image, and Citation Index   182

2. Notes   196

3. Bibliography   201

4. Index   205

5. Photo Credits   210

Foreword

Robert D. Leonard Jr.

James Zylstra, a student of traditional African money, has written an original inquiry into the nature of money itself with specific application to the "primitive" money of Africa, drawing on his experience as a teacher of mathematics in Nigeria in 1974–1978 for the Sudan United Mission, British Branch. Brimming with fascinating anecdotes, this little book places African primitive money in the context of African life.

Though not an exhaustive catalog, it provides an extensive survey of the major categories of African primitive money and their uses, with well-chosen illustrations. Zylstra considers the dual nature of much African primitive money—as ornament and valuable—and the difficulties encountered in actual use, because of the different types demanded in each local market. He suggests that primitive money persisted as long as it did because modern currency lacked religious and traditional value, and potentially spoiled the enjoyment of vigorous bargaining.

A particular interest of the author is the question of primitive money made by lost wax casting, in which he challenges earlier authorities on this subject.

Well-researched, *Primitive Money of Africa: Tales and Details* cites its sources and has an extensive bibliography.

Acknowledgments

A sincere debt of gratitude goes to the Hamill Gallery of Tribal Art in Boston, Massachusetts, for permission to use the poster that was adapted for the cover of this book. They also provided many illustrations from their photo gallery. Todd Zylstra, Dana Garlick, and Marilyn Zylstra acted as a steering committee helping to keep this ship on course. They assisted with far more than the mechanics of the process! Steve Zylstra, a nephew, handled the photography when it was needed. My hat is off to Marilyn Zylstra for the numerous sketches she drew of images that were otherwise not available. My editor, Keith Miller, was a great help in bringing the book to fruition. Without him the book would be considerably different. Thanks to others who gave encouragement when it was important.

Introduction

Though metal coins have been used since at least the seventh century BC, and the Roman Empire standardized currency in the fourth century BC, other forms of currency were prevalent in many locations. These included cowrie shells, stone discs, and beads. Some of these currencies were in use as recently as the middle of the twentieth century. Primitive money is a niche area within numismatics, but a highly interesting one.* This book examines primitive money in the African context.

Let's begin by asking what is *primitive* about the currency systems we'll be looking at. First, the currencies may not match with our standard notions. They might include farming tools that do not function as tools, shirts that are not designed to be worn, or throwing knives that lack a cutting edge. The uses to which this money applies may also be classified as primitive: paying off the medicine man for contacting your long-lost great-grandfather, or tying small bags of gold dust to the garment of a recently deceased relative just before burial.

Then there is the society in which this money has circulated. I spent a number of years in Nigeria, which provided an excellent social environment in which to understand the uses of primitive currency. For example, in chapter eleven you will read about a large tax office in Bauchi, a town in central Nigeria, where all employees, in the late

* There are those who prefer to use the terms "traditional money" or "odd and curious money." In this book, I will use the term "primitive money."

1940s, were assiduously counting cowrie shells. They would count the cowries, put them into bags, and then these bags would be packed on a donkey for transport—twenty thousand cowrie shells per donkey. In the 1970s I spent three years sixty-eight miles (110 km) southwest of Bauchi. I have seen some of those old government offices. I have seen traders in the local markets counting petty cash (modern coins then), and I have seen donkeys laden with goods. The time I spent in Africa enhanced my ability to describe the milieu in which this currency was used, in many places across the continent.

During the course of researching this book, numerous thoughts and questions arose. Can *any* item be an article of primitive money? After consulting a well-known authority concerning two mock shirts that I brought back from Nigeria, the answer was: "No, these items are not authentic primitive money." Later, after doing my own research and reviewing four of the foremost non-living authorities, I found credence to the status of the small and the large shirt: they were indeed primitive money from Nigeria. This shows not only the importance of doing good research, but also the lack of agreement among the authorities.

Next, there is an old question that has endured many years, which is whether any primitive money items were made using the cire perdue, or lost wax, process of casting. There is certainly an affinity, for example, between the brass lost-wax castings and the ironwork of a Bwaka throwing knife. Both required technical expertise, artistic ability, and the skills of the smith. This may lead us to imagine the possibility of a connection between primitive money and cire perdue. We'll look at this more closely in chapter seven.

Another philosophical issue is the relationship between primitive money and the articles of adornment or prestige items of status. The interest is in finding the catalyst that brought the two together. There are also the issues of the geographical, sociological, geological, and historical parameters of primitive money. Exactly how and where these variables came into play is important. Different villages adopted currencies with different characteristics: cloth, cowries, copper, and so on. What gave rise to the various characteristics? Lastly, when modern coinage was being introduced in many African countries, the governing officials attempted to force the people to convert from the established primitive currency to the new modern coinage. How cooperative were the people and the traders, and how successful was the government attempt to bring about this radical change? Chapter eleven deals with this issue, concentrating mostly on Nigeria and West Africa.

Details regarding the currency items may be found in the Data, Image, and Citation Index in the appendices. It is my sincere desire that you are delightfully entertained as you read these tales.

PART I
Tales

MOROCCO
ALGERIA
LIBYA
EGYPT
WESTERN SAHARA
TUNISIA
MAURITANIA
MALI
NIGER
SUDAN
CHAD
NIGERIA
SOUTH SUDAN
ETHIOPIA
SOMALIA
CAMEROON
CENTRAL AFRICAN REPUBLIC
GABON
CONGO
DEMOCRATIC REPUBLIC OF THE CONGO
UGANDA
KENYA
TANZANIA
ANGOLA
ZAMBIA
NAMIBIA
BOTSWANA
ZIMBABWE
MOZAMBIQUE
SOUTH AFRICA
MADAGASCAR
SENEGAL
GUINEA
BURKINA FASO
GHANA
CÔTE D'IVOIRE
BENIN
SIERRA LEONE
LIBERIA
THE GAMBIA
GUINEA-BISSAU
CAPE VERDE
EQUATORIAL GUINEA
SÃO TOMÉ AND PRÍNCIPE
COMOROS
SEYCHELLES
Northern Africa
Western Africa
Central Africa
Eastern Africa
Southern Africa

Money Matters

"Who covets more is evermore a slave." —ROBERT HERRICK

Boom box. In 1975, I visited a boarding school student of mine who lived with his parents in a remote village in Plateau State, Nigeria. We began our time together with the time-honored extended greetings in the Hausa language. After exchanging pleasantries for a short time, I told him I wanted to take a photograph of him in front of his father's hut. "Yes sir," he replied, and then paused. "But *Malam* [teacher], may I take just a moment first?" "Of course," I told him. He returned from his hut after a minute or two with a sizable (at least for 1975) portable boom box.

Fig. 1 Portable boom box from the 1970s

Now he was prepared for a photo. What he was saying was that he owned something of real value to himself, and if he owned it he must display it and even flaunt it. My student's action represented a Nigerian cultural principle that goes far back in time.

My student owned an object he wanted others to see and to know that he possessed. In much of Africa, men wanted part of their wealth to be displayed by their wives, or by themselves. These decorative items were legal tender accepted by the people, and in many cases were worn permanently. These currency items were worn around the wrists, arms, neck, or ankles, or several of those places simultaneously. They were generally made of iron, copper, brass, shells, beads, or ivory. Many were "valued for decoration as much as for use."[1]

Money definitions. Money can be defined as "a current medium of exchange in the form of coins and banknotes."[2] However, the concern in this book is primitive money, not coins and banknotes, and this definition says nothing of the basis of the currency. A broader definition would define money as "a commodity, such as gold or silver, that is legally established as an exchangeable equivalent of all other commodities and is used as a measure of their comparative values on the market."[3] The term *commodity* here refers to a basic raw material, product, or item that is useful in a monetary context. While primitive money was seldom legally established, it was an accepted, understood, and appreciated commodity. It was used by people who saw the need for and importance of this commodity in their community and accepted it for what it was. We shall look at diverse examples of this commodity from across Africa.

Functions of money. Money has four primary functions. First, money is primarily a *medium of exchange.* Money was used to purchase food. People exchanged money for items that were needed or desired. It was the medium by which they traded, and was very different from the bartering system that preceded it.

Second, money is a *store of value.* We can set it aside, save it, and use it later as it will retain or keep its value until a future date.

Third, money is a *standard of value* (sometimes referred to as a *unit of account*). It is a standard by which all things in the market are measured. From guinea corn to kola nuts, everything for sale in a market was measured by the same unit or standard. For example, one *mudu* of guinea corn might cost two Kissi pennies. In that case, Kissi pennies would be the unit. Other common standard units of exchange were cowrie shells and manillas.

Fig. 2 Kissi pennies: the money with a soul

Fig. 3 Individual cowrie shells along with two rotls

Fig. 4 Eight different common or trade manillas

Lastly, money is a *symbol of wealth.* That is why many Africans wore forms of money on their limbs, around their necks, or as decorative clothing items. If it wasn't displayed, it would be only a hidden symbol, so they showed it to others.

Characteristics of money. Our look at primitive money in Africa will be clarified even further if we observe the characteristics of modern Western currency and see if they match the characteristics of African primitive money. The first of those characteristics indicates that money should be *portable.* Here's a story that demonstrates this idea.

In the early 1890s, C. H. Robinson was in charge of an expedition in Hausaland, a large area of West Africa. One of the horses in the expedition became ill and would not be able to continue for many days. The issue was whether or not to sell the horse and continue the expedition. In that particular area, cowries were the primary unit of exchange. Upon doing the mathematics, Robinson discovered that when he found a buyer, he would have to hire fifteen extra porters to carry the money he received in exchange for the horse. These porters would earn the money they were carrying "plus a great deal more besides; there is in fact nothing which we could get in exchange for [the horse] which it would pay to carry with us."[4]

Fig. 5 All Maria Theresa thalers are dated 1780 after the date of her death.

Using cowries for large transactions could lead to serious problems. Interestingly, if the transaction had occurred in a larger village somewhere on the coast of West Africa, the Austrian Maria Theresa thalers would likely have been available. The value of Robinson's horse could then have been carried, as coin, in his pocket.

A simple purchase. A second characteristic is that money should be *homogeneous*, i.e., relatively uniform. Can one pass from one money form to another quite easily? Do the various components work well together as a system? The battleground for investigating this question is the village market, which was the major location of primitive money use in Africa. Were there any problems here with making purchases?

A story, again, will help to demonstrate the answer. A servant girl is sent to buy guinea corn in the Kukawa market in the kingdom of Bornu (today's northern Nigeria) in the 1850s. Note here the restrictions that are imposed on the girl as she tries to purchase guinea corn for her employer. Using Maria Theresa thalers, she first had to exchange these for cowrie shells at three thousand to the thaler, then was forced to find a trader who would exchange the cowries for a money form called a mock shirt. After all of that, it was back to the guinea corn trader to make her purchase using the mock shirt.

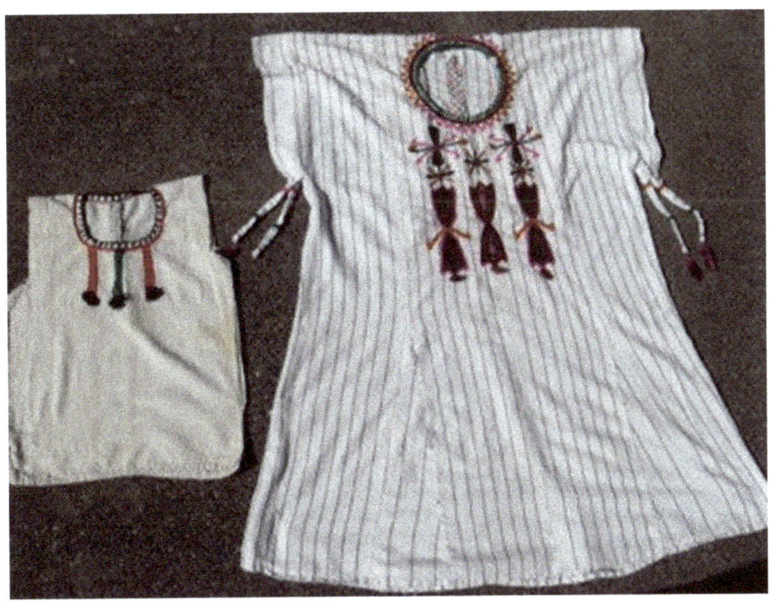

Fig. 6 Mock shirts, small and large, used mostly for market transactions.

Many traders would not accept just any of the primitive money commodities to complete the sale. It had to be the one that they favored. At this time the Maria Theresa thalers, the cowries, and the mock shirts were all considered valid currencies, and the guinea corn was a common grain in the markets. (Incidentally, mock shirts were not a common money unit throughout the continent. In northern Nigeria, they were cotton, sleeveless, impractical for wearing, and came in two sizes: tiny and very large. Today they are extremely rare and seldom seen in museums or galleries because of the deterioration factor.) This chain of the various currency exchanges that the servant girl went through could be long and complicated for someone looking for a common grain.

Interrelatedness. While the Kukawa market may not have been typical of all markets, it does expose a problem: making a purchase is not always easy. If we look at the class of iron hoes that were in use as a commodity in some Nigerian markets, we can see that they had a quality of interrelatedness. They came from the same iron bullion, many had a similar weight, and all had a similar labor-intensive quality. It should not be difficult, one would think, to relate one hoe to another in a transaction. But there was seldom more than one hoe in common use in a village.

Fig. 7 The cast iron round hoe blade was a symbol of agriculture.

Figs. 8 and 9 Left: The spade hoe symbolized life and death through food production and burial. Right: The cast iron narrow hoe was tribal money in Nigeria and Gabon.

The nine common manillas, which were copper bracelets used as currency, present a similar situation. They may appear interrelated, but they were seldom interchanged. Several were close in size, weight, and footprint, but the local traders insisted on their "chosen" manilla and each village market generally used its own manilla. They might not consider honoring any of the others, and would immediately identify only their one acceptable manilla.

The cowrie shells were almost always a welcome form of money, mostly because they were the smallest denomination and, as such, had a very important function.

Two conclusions can be drawn here: (1) every village market currency was different, or maybe even unique; and (2) common forms of a primitive currency were rare from one village to another.

In the West, our currency is good for anything where money is needed, from breakfast in a restaurant to the purchase of a new pair of shoes. We need not be concerned regarding the acceptance of it. The market in Kukawa had Maria Theresa thalers (unusual to find so far from the coastline) cowrie shells, mock shirts, and manillas. You could not assume that the adjacent villages had the same combination of primitive money in use in their markets, or even that a single form of currency was acceptable within one market. The same would be true of other uses of the money, whether they were used in paying tribute to a local chief, satisfying a court claim, or some other use. The lack of homogeneity was a problem that often occurred in conjunction with primitive money.

Durability. The third characteristic of money is that it should be *durable.* Just how resistant is primitive money to fire, rain, vandalism, or disease? There do not appear to be a large number of examples from the literature citing damages to this currency. However, we would have to assume that during the centuries when these money forms existed, the physical properties involved yielded some issues. The following are all primitive money examples from Africa with associated negative properties: salt melts, cattle are susceptible to disease, cotton cloth deteriorates rapidly in the tropics, cowrie shells and other shells can be crushed, and the flanged ends of the Kissi penny break off easily.

Cattle. Paul Einzig refers to the "cattle cult" among the Maasai in Kenya and Tanzania and the Wakamba in Kenya. To these people, goats and cattle were the principal currency, with a fixed ratio set between them, and with goats being considered "small change." Quality was unimportant, but quantity certainly was. They grossly overstocked the land, causing underfed cattle, soil erosion, and eventually deceased cattle. To understand the attitude of these cattle owners toward their cattle currency, we observe some simple "logic." The British agricultural expert Nigley Farson visited a farm and began arguing with some of the Wakamba about getting rid of some of their old and deceased cattle. One of them spoke up: "Listen, master—here are two pound notes. One is old and wrinkled and ready to tear—this one is a new one. But they are both worth a pound aren't they? Well, it's the same with cows. They are both a *cow*."[7] The number of "heads" was important so long as they were above ground. This indicates the durability of cattle currency.

Divisibility. Whether or not primitive money is *divisible* is the fourth characteristic. Most of the individual items were not easily divisible. However, there are examples of salt blocks being broken up, and "native cloth," strings of beads, and *rotls* were likewise divided. Rotls were strings of thirty-two cowries. Interestingly, they were often worth more as a rotl than as individual shells. Iron money could be converted to bullion or the bullion currency could be converted into an item such as Kissi pennies. This was not an easy transformation, but neither was it unusual. The only time cows were divided up was in the abattoir section of the village market!

Fig. 10 Nguni cattle

Recognizability. The fifth characteristic is that the money is *distinctive* or *recognizable*. Does the money have qualities that make it stand out in some way? Many of the beads and shells and bracelets certainly stood out, especially when they were worn decoratively.

Above: Fig. 11. An assortment of iron, brass and copper bracelets, all money items.

Below: Fig. 12. The Mbole hollow leg band is a popular item in museums and galleries.

The same is true of the copper and brass items such as the Mbole hollow leg band, which were shined nicely and worn on the ankle. Then there were a number of items that indicated status and wealth, and were designed to appear distinctive. These were all of the various spearheads, including the *liganda*, and a variety of throwing knives, which were borne by chiefs and village leaders. The large number of currency items that were made of iron had a high rank simply by virtue of the fact that they were made of iron.

Above left: Fig. 13 Ikonga spearhead, often used as a mark of status and for bride price. Right: Fig. 14 The Bangala spearhead had form, not function, for the tips were twisted.

Above left: Fig. 15 The Bwaka throwing knife shows form as well as function. Right: Fig. 16 The Mangbetu throwing knife was a mark of status and also a currency.

In the minds of the villagers, their primitive money made from iron was distinctive. The same was true in the Congo Basin, where copper items were the prominent commodity.

Stability. The last characteristic we shall look at is whether the money was *stable in value.* Whether the price for staple goods had a tendency to fluctuate in the village market is the question here. While there was no Federal Reserve Board to watch for signs of inflation, there were times when an appointed body did oversee the actions of a local market. In the case of Kano, located in what is now northern Nigeria, the emir set all of the prices in the entire market. More often it would be the tribal chief who assumed the jurisdiction of the economic affairs in the local market. Let's take a look at an example from West Africa.

Serious inflation. In 1868, 1869, and 1870 the port of Lagos, Nigeria, recorded 3,668 tons, 3,082 tons, and 2,769 tons, respectively, of cowries entering the port.[8] The value of the cowrie did show a variation from time to time and from one region to another, but it was stable enough to be the cornerstone of the currency system. However, what happened next is extraordinary. The cowrie could not stand up to the pressure put upon it in the 1880s, when several European countries sent 35,000 tons of cowrie shells to West Africa.

Immediately, inflation occurred. In some areas cowries were no longer used. In other areas it took decades to see much appreciation in its value. In the 1900s the government of Nigeria even banned the import of cowries, but they survived along with the other money forms.

Nevertheless, there was a reasonable *stability* in most primitive money systems. The stability existed because people had confidence in the value of the commodity. This confidence created the stability, and salt, cowries, and manillas were stable forms of currency for many centuries.

Uses of money. Barter was a common method of facilitating commerce in Africa before, during, and after the advent of primitive money there. However, the barter economy had a very serious limitation. A person may have wanted to exchange goods or services for an equivalent value of goods or services without the use of money; however, he or she may not have had on hand the acceptable goods or services to exchange. That is where the use of a commodity was such a logical solution. There is, however, one fact that is so very often ignored in this matter: there was a long period of time in African history where there was little need for the *use* of money. We simply don't think of the absence of that need. That is to say, a few centuries ago there was little emphasis placed on the importance of money. Each home was highly self-sufficient, and many homes did not require significant outside resources. Thus, the need for a currency system was not always very high. Here are some of the ways that primitive money was used in Africa:

1. Purchasing power in the local marketplace.
2. Satisfying court claims.
3. Paying tribute.
4. Compensating diviners and witch doctors.
5. Providing bridewealth.
6. Paying for burial ceremonies with help in the afterlife.
7. Setting a standard of value in the local economy.
8. Displaying social significance as jewelry and home decoration.
9. Exhibiting a mark of status and/or wealth in the community.
10. Purchasing slaves.

CHAPTER TWO
Money Milieu

"There are two things that can disrupt business in this country. One is war and the other is a meeting of the Federal Reserve." —WILL ROGERS

Milieu defined. A person's social environment.[1] The sphere, context, or setting in which a person lives.

Toward an appreciation of primitive money. In 1871, the journalist and explorer Henry M. Stanley made a seven-hundred-mile journey from Zanzibar to the interior of Africa, searching for the missionary explorer David Livingstone. Along the way, Stanley and his crew encountered extreme conditions and hardships. Transportation and communication facilities were basic.

Fig. 17 Sir Henry M. Stanley was an unusual explorer/journalist in Africa.

Fig. 18 Dr. David Livingstone, a pioneer medical missionary and explorer in Africa.

The compass and the machete, both of which had been around for centuries, were primary tools in their travels. However, there were no GPS guidance systems, no drones with cameras, no smartphones . . . indeed, there were no "dumb" phones!

Though the telegraph had been invented, it was not in use in central Africa. Communication was oral, in-person, and required a translator to cross language barriers. There were numerous languages and dialects to contend with. What additional problems did Stanley face?

Fig. 19 The magnetic compass is an instrument for navigation from the 11th century.

The selection of the form of currency. The expedition was sponsored by the *New York Herald* and consisted of 192 people in five caravans. "Altogether," Stanley wrote, "the expedition numbers three white men, twenty-two soldiers, four supernumeraries, with a transport train of eighty-two pagazis, twenty-seven donkey and two horses, conveying fifty-two bales of cloth, seven man-loads of wire [*cheetem*], sixteen man-loads of beads, twenty loads of boat fixtures, three loads of tents, four loads of clothes and personal baggage, two loads of cooking utensils and dishes, one load of medicines, three of powder, five of bullets, small shot and metallic cartridges, three of instruments and small necessaries, such as soap, sugar, tea, coffee, Liebig's extract of meat, pemmican, candles etc., which makes a total of one hundred sixteen loads—equal to eight and a half tons of material."[2] All of the soldiers had defensive work as well as serving in other ways on the expedition. The four supernumeraries were hired not as regular staff but as special staff to do translation work and lend credence to the *Herald* expedition in the eyes of the village chiefs. The *pagazis* were porters who carried loads on their heads or on their shoulders, eighty pounds being their maximum. The cloth, wire, and beads were the cash to be used for payroll, food, and tribute to the chiefs whose territory they passed through. The problem with all the cash and supplies is that when the pagazis or others decided to abandon the expedition, they were also tempted to steal from their benefactor. If they wanted to run away, they would not do so empty-handed. It was all a part of the difficulty in African travel.

Where possible, canoes or small boats were used in travel. This is why Stanley included twenty loads of boat parts. Before he departed, a boat was designed that could be disassembled and hand-carried on land until needed. Efforts were made to confront all imaginable hardships.

Cloth, wire, and beads. In Nigeria alone, there were numerous examples of "native" cloth, each with its own name. They had different dimensions and different colors: white, black, gray, indigo, blue, and orange, sometimes striped and sometimes solid. There were many places where "mat money" was used, called Kuba cloth or raffia cloth. This could have been a part of the fifty-two bales carried by the porters of the Stanley expedition. It is possible that the imported calico may also have been a candidate for a part of the currency that Stanley selected. The reference to wire as currency was almost certainly to cheetem (also called *sitim* and *usitim*), which was common in southern Nigeria.

Above left: Fig. 20 Cloths were strips of cotton, here sewn together for a blanket. Right: Fig. 21 Cheetem was the wire currency that Stanley brought along.

In chapter one we learned that money should be distinctive. Many of the beads were just that. The true aggry bead was different shades of blue, and was used as currency in Ghana, Benin, and Nigeria.

Fig. 22 The tubular aggry bead became valuable as currency.

The beautiful millefiori beads were of varying lengths, shapes, and colors, and were found throughout much of Africa. The elbow shape (below) was the most valuable.

Fig. 23 A millefiori bead was a Venetian glass bead, tubular in shape and colorful.

The Hebron beads were green, yellow, and occasionally black and blue, and were around for centuries in the area between the Sudan and Nigeria.

Fig. 24 Hebron beads came from the Dead Sea area.

The tiny, attractive Munshi beads were made of brass, and originated with the Munshi (Tiv) tribe in Nigeria.

Fig. 25 Munshi beads were worn as jewelry and also used to buy slaves.

The Turkana tribe in Kenya and Uganda made ostrich eggshell beads as necklaces, which have been around since 7,000 BC.

Fig. 26. Ostrich eggshell beads were also called "bushmen's beads" in Namibia.

These were also used in North Africa for a time. Stanley's expedition carried sixteen total man-loads of beads, which translates to well over half a ton of beads. That is a great deal of money!

Doing the math. If we were to do the math regarding the primitive money carried by the Stanley expedition, we would find that 75 loads out of a total of 116 loads consisted of money. That represents 65 percent of the total. In addition, the area through which Stanley and the expedition traveled (from Zanzibar to Ujiji in what is now Tanzania) had no established "medium of exchange or unit of value,"[2] although Stanley was unaware of this. The conclusion to his money problem was that all of those loads of money he was transporting may have had little use to him. He could use it to barter, but with no guarantee of success.

Connecting the dots. Philosophically, is there any further reason to mention the issues related to an explorer who is searching for a medical missionary turned explorer by the name of Dr. Livingstone?

And what is the connection of all of this to primitive money? Had we been living at this time in 1871, our response would be: "Yes! It is important to study the issues as to where Dr. Livingstone is located." The reason for this response is that there was no subject more commonly on the minds and lips of the average world citizen. There was no human individual that the world found more exciting than Dr.

Livingstone. He was headline news. That is why the *New York Herald* financed the expedition. They wanted the scoop. Livingstone was himself, at the time, searching for the source of the Nile River but had not been heard from in years. Was he alive or dead? Was he still searching for the source of the Nile?

Fig. 27 Henry M. Stanley meets Dr. Livingstone, a very remarkable African story.

The world desperately wanted an answer. Now, the answer to the other question—how is this all related to primitive money?—will take a little explanation.

A few questions. Can one be a collector of Greek and Roman coins without studying classical antiquity? Can one learn to appreciate primitive money without studying the context and the time period under which this money was in use? The point here is that the more we learn about the social context, the more we may appreciate the study of primitive money.

Henry M. Stanley provided some of that context in the preceding story. In Europe there was a frenzy of activity in many of the capitals following the popular notion that an expansion into Africa, "the Dark Continent" (a phrase coined by Stanley), was important. Most European countries were fascinated with this issue.

A few absurdities. It is ironic that the Victorian Age of 1837–1901 coincided so closely with the colonial expansion period in Africa. It was the Victorian sensibilities: highly moralistic, straitlaced behavior, along with peace and prosperity, versus the African survivor culture: typhoid, malaria, drowning, attack by wild animals, dysentery, and scurvy. Ludicrous, is it not, to think of the dozens of Europeans who left their armchairs in exchange for the "glamorous life" of the African "discoverers"? As the leaders of the expeditions, it was their lot to determine when to halt, when to continue, when to change direction, when to fight, when to eat, and when to negotiate—quite likely with the use of their primitive currency. The animals were not always friendly, and neither were the tribal chiefs. During Henry Stanley's second expedition, to map the Congo River, he was engaged in a total of thirty-two battles.[4] Desertion was another constant issue. For example, Verney Lovett Cameron, leader of an expedition in 1873, hired two hundred porters. Many of the porters deserted early on, however, because he made the mistake of paying his men before departure.[5] Another well-known explorer, John Hanning Speke, departed from Zanzibar in 1860 with seventy-six porters and arrived at his destination with eighteen.[6] That is a decrease of 76 percent! Think of the constant reorganization they must have experienced as an expedition.

Courage and daring. All of these explorers left the comforts of their home culture, some taking a few comforts with them. Several started out with their wives, but sent them back soon after arrival in Africa. A few even took beds with them. The national flag, representing the home country, was carried at the head of the long column.[7]

Fig. 28 Theodore Roosevelt's expedition; Stanley's would also have included a U.S. flag.

The exception was when the trailblazers were at the head of the column. Keep in mind that this body of people is traveling in a foreign country, often in a hostile context, at the mercy of tribal chiefs, wild animals, and unknown village leaders. Diseases and accidents were a real deterrent to their progress.

When the explorers returned to their native land, it was invariably to great acclaim. They were invited to formal dinners and official meetings, and showered with honors, medals, and awards. However, the indispensable African rowers, scouts, interpreters, guides, cooks, and porters were seldom recognized at these events.[8]

The milieu. In this chapter, we have immersed ourselves in the African environment by observing various European explorers in Africa. This milieu should help us to better understand and appreciate the primitive money that was in use at that time. The individual money items that we read about here are not isolated hunks of copper, brass, iron, tin, shell, ivory, or cloth. There is a history and a tale behind each item, and they were used within specific cultural and social contexts. We look next at the cultural characteristics that were present at the time these monies were in use.

Cultural characteristics during the primitive money era. During the primitive money period there were no written languages in sub-Saharan Africa. The lack of written records had a major effect on the research that is available. European explorers, missionaries, and traders in Africa, as well as historians, have pieced together the history of the region.

African culture at this time had five primary characteristics. First, it was *patriarchal*, i.e., controlled by men. This control or domination will be noticed throughout this book. The exception is the environment of the village market. The women were often the traders as well as the buyers, while the men stayed under the shade of the baobab tree, sharing talk and kola nuts with friends.

Second, a *subsistence economy* characterizes the earlier part of this period. Only the bare necessities were available. There was no notion of capitalism yet, and no cash crop was anticipated. They farmed for food to feed themselves and, if necessary, to help their neighbors. It was not a truck farm. No discretionary funds were in the family budget.

Third, *life was rudimentary*. Just the basics. Carry the water you need in the morning. Bathe in the river while you wash the clothes. Life was simple: there was no power and no running water, unless you lived by a stream.

Fourth, *there was a self-sufficient family unit*. Mother and children were involved in tilling the soil, growing food, drawing water, pounding yams, and washing clothes. The father did some of the heavy tilling, but the mother was the key in this cohesive unit: the glue holding the family together.

Fifth, there were *close tribal ties.* As an outward indication of these ties, many tribes had a distinctive tribal mark that was placed on the flesh of the face of newborn babies or during adolescence. It remained for life. Beyond this tribal mark, the tribe generally passed animistic beliefs and other traditions on to all members.

The last descriptive characteristic was a *survival mentality.* Children learned at an early age that they were drawing water for a reason, they were pulling weeds on the family farm plot for a reason, and they were carrying messages to their uncle in a neighboring village for a reason. Everyone knew that they played a role in keeping the family, village, and tribe afloat.

A survival mentality. This struggle was demonstrated to me on a personal level while I was living in a rather remote location in Plateau State, Nigeria, in 1977. Two young boys often walked by my home on their way from elementary school. Luka and John may have been about eleven or twelve years old, and I was able to form a relationship with them. One day an idea came to me. I decided to give them a few rabbits, including a male and a female, that I had started raising, intending to eat the offspring. I asked the boys if they were interested in raising rabbits. I can still see their affirmative response with bright eyes and broad smiles.

Fig. 29 Luka, John, two cages, and a few rabbits. Note the *abinci zomo* on head.

I gave them a few words about *abinci zomo* (food for rabbits) and the gestation period for rabbits. One afternoon after school, two very happy boys left my home, "hopping" down the path with two rabbits in a cage.

This tale does not have a happy ending, however. Two weeks later, I again saw them walking by my place. They were obviously downcast. I asked the question that I could probably have guessed the answer to. Yes, they had eaten them all!

Metaphor, hyperbole, circumlocution, and repetition. Another important component of the milieu is language. If our goal here is to try to "experience" the context where the primitive money was used, we must include language in that mix. The following are humorous accounts that impart some of the flavor in communicating at various levels and in various countries in Africa in the latter part of the nineteenth century.

Mary H. Kingsley, the British writer and explorer, describes a scene in which she is in the presence of two people: King Coffee, the head of the Kruboys (the crew hired to offload a ship), and the captain of the ship. The captain has decided to pay the Kruboys in silver coin instead of the usual crates of gin, because he thought Mary was a temperance missionary and he didn't want to offend her. She writes: "King Coffee's face was a study. If Captain X, whom he knew of old, had stood on his head and turned bright blue all over with yellow spots before his eyes, it would not have been anything like a shock. 'What for good him ting, Cappy?' he asked. 'What for good him ting for we country? I suppose you gib gin, tobacco, gun, he be fit for trade, but money . . .' Here his Majesty's feelings flew ahead of the royal command of language, great as that was, and he expectorated with profound feeling and expression."[9]

In this story, King Coffee is offended, saying that the captain could pay in many acceptable ways, but to offer foreign silver coins was an insult. As we will learn in chapter five, gin was legal tender in both Ghana and Nigeria at this time.

This came about when Europe produced cheap iron and sent it to West Africa. This had the effect of depreciating the iron bar, another currency, and replacing it with a case of gin. It was on par, a case of gin to one iron bar. King Coffee wasn't the only one who had a great dislike for modern coinage. This will come up again.

Fig. 30 European traders brought in inferior-quality iron bars as money.

"With most profoundly . . ." The following account is a letter from eleven women from a modest-sized Nigerian village, to the "authorities."

Sir,

With most profoundly, we have the honor respectfully to approach your very worship.

Sir, We native of—Igbara woman greatly surprise to put before you and to explain to your kind and solute consideration.

Sir, We beg to ask you to give us your ears and with deep thoughts.

Sir, We citizens of the country—and not denizens has the pleasure to acquaint with your kind favor to make you to understand for us, though we are ignorant and illeterate before you but not in this point, we want your help now.

Sir, From our great grand Generation the fore parents we have our very native customary chop meantime is our drink which brings the strength to our husbands the farmers more and more, and gives chop to our country aboundantly which named the—fruitful country.

Sir, This our food describing is Guinea corn which yourself can identify same by given to your horse how powerful you real seeing in it ?

Sir, We native woman when cooked this Guinea corn for drink and our native men as their customary drink, put in the calabash pot or bottle called Kolia with them to farm it gives there power to work.

Sir, This Guinea corn drink called Pito gives also strength to our old aged men and women who has no teeth and strength jaws to chew food is only their chop.

Sir, This now we are not allowed to use our native fooding which wiil give us native and none natives cheapest food like formerly, all the coasters can witness that chops are not so cheap as before, owing to what sir, Owing to the lack of this Pito when people can't get to their farms.

Sir, This prohibition of our native chop Guinea corn by the Government or the Authority in charge——our born country, we made to understand that it was the advise from the denizen chief of——who is not our born land man, he has determined to turn our country upside down, but we natives beg your worship to regenerate our country into former condition especial with our chop which is our drink, also.

Sir, we wish to get this denizen chief who is ruin our country in your court to let him know who he is in——.

Sir, We again beg to notice you that we shall soon want of plenty food if Railway business reach to our border therefore we need sufficient to help us in our farms that Guinea corn using in chopping and drinking as Pito.

We are yours Obedient Maid Servants

A   E   J
B   F   K

    C   G   L

    D   H

Pl. Sir, We are more than this numbers 11"[10]

We can sum up the women's request in four words: "We want our beer!"

The well-known Nigerian journalist and author Peter Enahoro made an appropriate comment regarding Nigerian oratory: "The power of Nigerian oratory is measured by the strength of the speaker's legs. This is not a Nigerian proverb, but it ought to be."[11]

CHAPTER THREE

Money in the Market

"Money may not buy love, but it sure can add zest to the shopping."
—HENNY YOUNGMAN

The very heartbeat of the village. As noted earlier, most primitive money in Africa was used in the marketplace. I'm going to transport you to the marketplace of an average-sized West African village in the latter half of the nineteenth century.

Fig. 31 The local market. If we could only experience the sights, sounds, and smells!

The market day was generally once per week. At one end of a large plot of ground, the goat and sheep sales occur. There may be an abattoir close by where cattle are slaughtered in an open-air setting. Yes, there are flies and an odor of urine—human and animal. Permeating the air are also the odors of cooking food, burning wood, and human perspiration. Vultures love to congregate here. Barking dogs run loose, competing with the vultures for scraps, though there aren't many of those. Nothing is wasted at the abattoir—even the intestines are used.

Walking on, we see concentrations of traders selling fabrics, then a large group selling grains, and then a concentration of women with small fires and cooking utensils selling prepared food amid much smoke.

No "bankers' hours" here. Somewhere in all of this maze, there may be a money-changer, "who sits on a mat with a pile of irons in front of him."[1] "Irons" here may refer to any number of items made of iron, including the *tajere* (also called *losol*), *idoma*, *dubil*, and *purr-purr*.

Fig. 32 The tajere was an iron bar currency sometimes made into farming tools

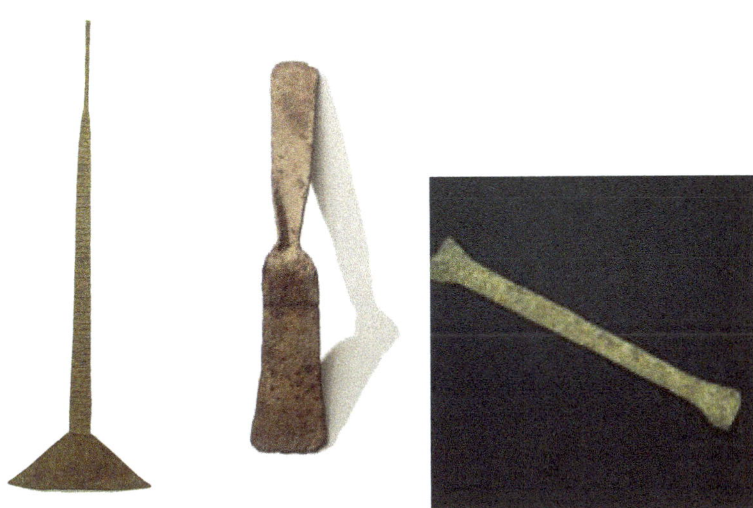

Above left: Fig. 33 Another hoe currency with an unusual shape was the idoma. Middle: Fig. 34 The purr-purr was used in larger transactions, ceremonies and bride price. Right: Fig. 35 The dubil was an iron bar currency in NE Nigeria sometimes used in bride price.

Iron hoes, of which there are several varieties, including the narrow hoe, round hoe, and spade hoe, are also referred to as irons. There are a number of currency items, also made of iron, that are of lower denomination that our money changer may have available: Kissi pennies, needle money, and Ogoja pennies, for example.

Fig. 36 Needle money. In fourteenth-century Ethiopia it took 5,000 of these iron needles to buy a cow.

Some of these currencies are found only in small areas of the continent. Needle money was used in Ethiopia and Nigeria, and was half an inch in length. It had twice the value of cowrie shells. Ogoja pennies were Y-shaped currency used in several states in Nigeria. They were eight to eleven inches in length. Toward the end of the primitive money era their value became less than a halfpenny.

Fig. 37 Ogoja penny. These Y-shaped iron pieces were used in the DRC and Nigeria.

Along with the irons, our money-changer may also have had cowrie shells, trade beads, brass or copper rods, straw tin, cloths, and manillas. The use of straw tin was limited to the area where the tin was mined: the large Jos Plateau, Nigeria.

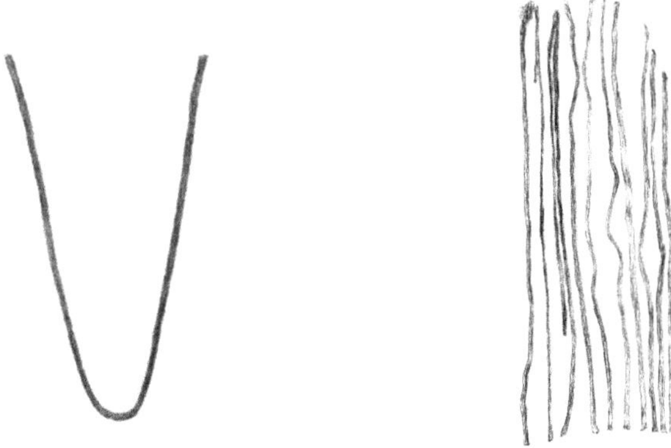

Above left: Fig. 38 Calabar rods: these quarter-inch, U-shaped brass or copper rods are about one yard long.
Right: Fig. 39 Straw tin were strips of pure tin and were small change in the marketplace.

The money changer may well have had whatever the need was in that market, but it was not a certainty. Not enough markets had a money changer, but if they did, he was important in helping to make a purchase.

A typical Ibo market. The Ibo people are a very large tribe with an interesting history. They are energetic, intelligent, and bold in their thinking. They were one of the primary groups involved in the export of slaves. They conducted many slave raids and were very successful. This tradition worked against them, however, when they tried to separate from the Federal Republic of Nigeria in the Biafran War in 1967. They were a persecuted tribe before, during, and after the civil strife. However, in the early 1900s, their markets tended to be very productive and well-organized institutions.

Most average-sized Ibo villages had a marketplace. Some villages also had joint markets on certain days for the convenience of the people. These tended to be located close to the main thoroughfare passing through the village. As it was the responsibility of the younger boys to see that the market was swept before each market day, they arrived at the break of dawn. Shortly thereafter, the vendors began to arrive. The early birds got the choice of the best shady spots available. Some may have provided limited shade of their own. They all knew just where the various categories of goods were situated: grains, produce, meats, baskets, mats, fabrics, live chickens, pots, tools, and the imported goods from Europe. The live goats and sheep were also available in a grassy location some distance away, where they could graze.[2]

A chicken on one leg. The cost of a laying hen in the early 1900s may have been around 650 cowries, or the equivalent of 14 US pennies at the time. Remember, however, that buyers in Africa don't really know the cost until they haggle or negotiate. This may take some time; you do not rush the process. If perchance you discredit the chicken because it stands on only one leg, you have just extended the negotiation. That is considered an offensive act, and it will not go unchallenged. The seller's voice will be raised in defense of the chicken, and the vendor in the neighboring stall will come to the aid of the chicken seller and with an even louder voice will tell you just what you do not know about chickens. Then others in the wider area will give their opinions, and you eventually realize that you may not find the chicken available for 650 cowries after all, no matter how long you haggle. Remember, though, that there are plenty of other chickens available—on one leg or two—and this is an all-day affair.

Husbands are like male spiders. The markets in Accra, Ghana, at the end of the nineteenth century, were remarkable for several reasons. They were large, vigorous, and had a set of astute women traders—at that time referred to as mammies—who were highly engaged and focused. They were large-boned, strong as buffalos, and strident, and were dressed gaily for a long day. They were a determined and long-suffering lot. These women had recently learned an important principle of capitalism: you can put money aside for a rainy day. It is possible to earn money over and above your needs for the essentials of life. The British author Richard Fry describes them: "Their god is money and they adore him constantly. They are down at their stalls by six in the morning and stay until dark. . . . Somewhere a husband is working, idling, or trading too. These husbands are, in a sense, adjuncts, like male spiders; it is the market women who make the money and call the tune."[3]

Although most of these female vendors were, at that time, illiterate, they carried so much information in their heads that they did very well financially, and had a good reputation with the trading companies from whom they purchased much of their goods. Often, the trading companies did not even know their addresses, and yet it was very rare for one of the market women to default.

One size does not fit all. The Lele were a large, unusual tribe situated between the Kasai and Loange rivers in what is now the Democratic Republic of Congo. In 1950 they occupied many villages, with an average size of 190 inhabitants and a density of 4 persons per square mile. These villages had no markets and were for the most part self-sufficient entities based on subsistence agriculture. They did not use legal tender; rather, they used a very complex system of "gifting." The individual family units were very strong, but they used one very important communal activity that demonstrated teamwork and a cooperative effort. Periodically, every able-bodied man from the village would participate in the communal hunt. The meat and hide from the hunt were shared according to cult membership obligations.

Gifting. This gifting idea was the key to the village economic system, and was based on the manufacture and distribution of raffia cloth, woven from the fibers of the raffia palm tree leaves. Raffia cloth, also called Kuba cloth, mat money, or madiba, is coarse but attractive. It was not intended to be sold but rather to be presented as gifts. As Mary Douglas explains: "Every man and boy can weave. The preparation of materials for weaving is long and the actual work of weaving is more arduous than might be supposed."[4] Once his loom is set up, an adult male can weave two to three lengths in a day if he works steadily. Five lengths is the output of a very fast worker. Two lengths sewn together made a skirt for a woman or a man (these were rather delicate, and only lasted about four months). Ten lengths sewn together with a rich appliqué border formed a dance skirt called *mapel mahangi*, a prized heirloom. Informal gifts of raffia cloth were made to smooth all social relations: husband to wife, son to mother, son to father, and so on. These gifts might take place during times of tension, as peace offerings, as parting gifts, or in order to convey congratulations. There were also formal gifts, which were neglected only at the risk of a rupture of important social ties. For example:

- A male on reaching adulthood would give twenty cloths to his father. He knew that he would soon need his father's help in raising bride-price.

- A husband gave twenty cloths to his wife for each delivery of a child. This qualified him as eligible for entrance into a cult group. If he didn't, she might repudiate the marriage.

- The husband should bury each of his wife's parents with a mortuary gift of twenty cloths.
- If a wife reported a would-be seducer, her virtue should be rewarded with twenty cloths.

There was a complex system of gifts, fees, fines, damages, and compensations, which could go toward the acquisition, restoration, and maintenance of community status. This "gifting" could also be used toward the obligation of damages for adultery, admission to cults, tribute to chiefs, and obligations to diviners. It was not considered a medium of exchange when used within the village. The important idea in the Lele community was the notion of acquiring status. Goods (raffia cloths) were "distributed mostly on the basis of status, and not by purchase."[5] The lack of any markets or medium of exchange makes the Lele tribe considerably different from any of the other tribal communities that we have thus far observed.

Fig. 40 Raffia cloth (also known as kuba cloth or mat money) was made from the leaves of raffia palm.

Not to panic. In Kano, Nigeria, one of the older cities in all Africa, an incident occurred that is worth mentioning. The year was 1975 and the market in Kano covered a large area. The stalls were close together, the aisles narrow, and the sights, sounds, and smells were all quite normal. Normal enough for my eight-year-old son to wander off and do some exploring on his own. He had blond hair and light skin, and he should have been easy to spot weaving in and out of the clusters of people. Not so. I turned from making a purchase, and he'd disappeared.

But don't panic! This market was, at that time, friendly and safe enough. The solution used was to find a young local boy who wanted to earn a little money, and give him a shilling to begin the search and a shilling upon delivery. (In 1975, primitive money was no longer actively used.) The boy, who knew the market well, was hired and within fifteen minutes he delivered my son to me. Another shilling was produced. Parents were delighted, son was fine, and the local boy, sometime called a *bamboi* in Hausa, was rewarded with two shillings.

The Duketown market. Duketown was the capital of Old Calabar in southern Nigeria, and had two marketplaces. Market was held every day, but alternated between the two locations. The larger one was on a hill and is here described by Thomas J. Hutchinson, British Consul.

"The first impression that one has on coming within sight of it, and hearing of the murmur in the vastness of negro life before you, is that all the females of the adjoining countries have met for a gabbling party, with the intention of trying to talk one another to death. Amongst the several hundred persons in the market-place, it may be inferred at once, from the clatter, that the softer sex have a predominance, both as venders and purchasers. The currency among them consists of pieces of copper wire, blackened and bent into a horse-shoe form, called 'black coppers' [likely cheetem]. Bundles of fire-wood, nuts of the palm tree, cocoa nuts, oranges, pineapples—and in their season cassava, cocoa root, lanterns, bananas, and Indian corn,—elephant's flesh, living goats, fowls, and eggs, with a variety of British manufactured goods, constitute the articles offered for sale. There are no tables or standings to place these upon. Such as would receive detriment from coming in contact with the ground, are contained in calabashes, and the seller squats down beside them.

"But try to push your way through the crowd, and the exhaling odour from that naked congregation almost paralyses you. Men and women in Old Kalabar wear no clothing, save a hip-swathe, differing in its material with the difference of the wearer's rank and station. Here, in this market-place, there is palpable evidence of the condition of affairs arising from this practice. No vile compound of drugs or chemicals—the vilest that could be fabricated by human ingenuity—would rival the perspiratory stench from the assembled multitude. It is not only tangible to the olfactory nerves, but you feel conscious of its permeating the whole surface of your body. Even after going from the sphere of its generation, it hovers about you and sticks to your clothes, and galls you to such an extent that, with stick and umbrella in your hands, you try to beat it off, feeling as if it were an invisible fiend endeavoring to become assimilated with your life-blood."[6]

"Primitive markets constitute the principal means of entertainment."[7] Spending money in the local marketplace can test your sense of smell, sense of humor, level of patience, and ability to bargain. A "marketplace compromise purchase" is fascinating to observe and actually fun to participate in. The key word is *compromise*. Prices are not shown anywhere; it is up to the vendor to determine the price. As Nigerian journalist Peter Enahoro puts it: "In most parts of the world, a price tag tells you the exact cost of an article on display in a market. Not so in Nigeria. There are no price tags; although there are prices."[8] If you need three eggs for breakfast, you ask the vendor what the cost will be. She knows that the price is twenty-eight cowries but will ask for thirty-one cowries. You, the buyer, know that the price is twenty-eight cowries so you offer twenty-five cowries. The vendor has gone three over and you have gone three under. You haggle for several minutes, you laugh and you joke, you sometimes even put a serious expression on your face, and finally—surprise, you have reached a compromise! You hear the words, "Bring your money." Success at twenty-eight cowries. It is all a part of the system; just enjoy it and don't take it all too seriously.

Prolonged bargaining is loved. Indeed, the African does love prolonged bargaining. It is seen as a personal challenge; a one-on-one game of *mancala,* in which their love of talking rapidly with much gesticulation can be perfected.* The traders in this exchange exert themselves, throwing themselves into the role of the super salesman.

Fig. 41 Mancala is one of the oldest board games in the world.

They have great enthusiasm and unfailing confidence in their ability to see success in the transaction. The non-African observing all of this is still attempting to acclimate to the sights, sounds, and smells, and may also be trying to stay out of the way of the vendors' goods coming through the crowd with loads balanced on rapidly moving heads. The experience is a slight contrast to visiting the local Walmart or stopping off at the corner Starbucks for a morning coffee while on the way to work.

* Mancala, sometimes called *ayo ayo, warri,* or *oware,* is a pit-and-pebble game that originated in the Sudan 3,600 years ago. Some call it the national game of Africa.

Fixed-value currency. As we have seen, the village market was traditionally the center of commerce in Africa. At the beginning of the twentieth century, though, change was in the air. European and even American coinage started to enter the markets along the coastal areas of Africa. However, many did not want to see silver, copper, and nickel coinage emerge in their markets. They saw coins as fixed-value currency permitting a rapid sale that might limit the extended bargaining concept that was common in their markets, taking away the immense enjoyment they had experienced for centuries. Further, the African felt that modern coinage lacked the magico-religious virtue that their own primitive currency had. King Coffee, mentioned earlier, had the right idea: modern coinage is not necessarily good. After all, "What for good him ting for we country, Cappy?"[9] There will be more on this later.

CHAPTER FOUR

Money and Marriage

"The payment for a wife is still the feature that distinguishes licit from illicit marriage." —A. HINGSTON QUIGGIN

Something was amiss. "Are we there yet, Dad?" Before giving a waffling answer to my six-year-old son, I had to ask myself three questions. The first: "Is this village, at the end of this rocky, two-track road, the right village where the wedding is to be held?" The second: "Is it the correct time and day for the wedding?" The third: "Was this trip necessary?" The answer to all three questions was "Yes." This was Nigeria, where road signs were uncommon, where small villages might not be identified, and where you often found yourself reading the "unwritten signs" that were so important. The unwritten sign here was a lack of foot traffic or vehicles for a wedding that was to be held at the only church in sight. It was quiet and desolate. No one was around. Something was amiss.

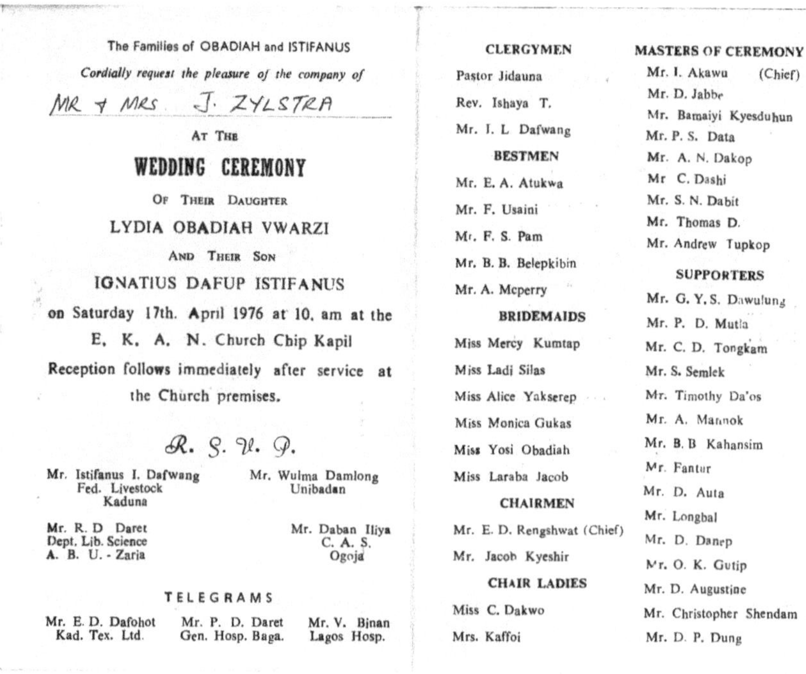

The Families of OBADIAH and ISTIFANUS

Cordially request the pleasure of the company of

MR & MRS   J. ZYLSTRA

AT THE

WEDDING CEREMONY

OF THEIR DAUGHTER

LYDIA OBADIAH VWARZI

AND THEIR SON

IGNATIUS DAFUP ISTIFANUS

on Saturday 17th. April 1976 at 10, am at the
E. K. A. N. Church Chip Kapil

Reception follows immediately after service at
the Church premises.

R. S. V. P.

Mr. Istifanus I. Dafwang
Fed. Livestock
Kaduna

Mr. Wulma Damlong
Unibadan

Mr. R. D Daret
Dept. Lib. Science
A. B. U. - Zaria

Mr. Daban Iliya
C. A. S.
Ogoja

TELEGRAMS

Mr. E. D. Dafohot
Kad. Tex. Ltd.

Mr. P. D. Daret
Gen. Hosp. Baga.

Mr. V. Binan
Lagos Hosp.

CLERGYMEN

Pastor Jidauna

Rev. Ishaya T.

Mr. I. L Dafwang

BESTMEN

Mr. E. A. Atukwa

Mr. F. Usaini

Mr. F. S. Pam

Mr. B. B. Belepkibin

Mr. A. Mcperry

BRIDEMAIDS

Miss Mercy Kumtap

Miss Ladi Silas

Miss Alice Yakserep

Miss Monica Gukas

Miss Yosi Obadiah

Miss Laraba Jacob

CHAIRMEN

Mr. E. D. Rengshwat (Chief)

Mr. Jacob Kyeshir

CHAIR LADIES

Miss C. Dakwo

Mrs. Kaffoi

MASTERS OF CEREMONY

Mr. I. Akawu   (Chief)

Mr. D. Jabbe

Mr. Bamaiyi Kyesduhun

Mr. P. S. Data

Mr. A. N. Dakop

Mr C. Dashi

Mr. S. N. Dabit

Mr. Thomas D.

Mr. Andrew Tupkop

SUPPORTERS

Mr. G. Y. S. Dawulung

Mr. P. D. Mutla

Mr. C. D. Tongkam

Mr. S. Semlek

Mr. Timothy Da'os

Mr. A. Mannok

Mr. B. B Kahansim

Mr. Fantur

Mr. D. Auta

Mr. Longbal

Mr. D. Danep

Mr. O. K. Gutip

Mr. D. Augustine

Mr. Christopher Shendam

Mr. D. P. Dung

Fig. 42 Most of the participants at the wedding are shown on the opposite side.

Bride-price. What was amiss was the ceremony. The people were not there because there was no reason for them to be there. The ceremony did not begin because there was one final act that had to occur before the bride would be available. The father of the groom and the father of the bride had to renegotiate the bride-price. At the time, when a young girl was selected as a bride for a son, the father of the groom was expected to pay generously in a negotiated settlement to the father of the bride for the loss of her services to him. Westerners call this a "bride-price." There were numerous variations of this throughout the continent of Africa, and the custom had been around for centuries.

The renegotiation. The renegotiation took a good two hours. Waiting in separate compounds, the adult males were seated in a circle and served *kunu*, a fermented guinea corn drink, in a small calabash. When the negotiations were completed, we were ushered into a small sixty-person chapel where we continued to wait. Eventually, a procession came into view, walking down the beaten-earth path. The chapel could not hold all the attendees, so many were outside, looking in the windows and doors. The ceremony finally began and everything proceeded smoothly. No announcement was made concerning the details of the renegotiation.

"The production of iron was a cult act."[1] In 1976, the bride-price may well have consisted primarily of food items: rice, guinea corn, kola nuts, local palm wine, chickens, sheep, goats, and, if possible, cattle. Prior to 1948, however, it was likely a very different kind of settlement. At that time, items of primitive money constituted the bride-price. One class of these money items consisted of objects made of iron. Iron production was a cult act by the smelters (more on this in chapter six). Iron had a mystique associated with it. Whether it was fashioned into ceremonial money in the shape of a gong or a liganda, or one of the currency hoes that Nigeria was known for, iron loomed large in connection to bride-price. Iron was a medium of exchange, a symbol of wealth, and a standard of value. Ceremonial gongs were currency in a swath from Togo all the way to East Africa, including Benin, Nigeria, Cameroon, Central African Republic, the Democratic Republic of Congo, Uganda, Kenya, and Tanzania.

The liganda could buy a canoe. The liganda, also called *ngbele*, was used by the Topoke tribe on the Lomami River in the Democratic Republic of Congo. The larger its size, the more prestigious it was and the greater was its purchasing power. The one shown here is only four feet ten inches, but some were longer than five feet ten inches.

Fig. 43 The liganda, made of sheet iron, came in three denominations.

Hoes, as currency, were found in West Africa and the Congo Basin in the Democratic Republic of Congo. Kissi pennies, called *kilindi* in some areas, were also common in the bride-price package in Liberia, Guinea, and Sierra Leone. These are pieces of long, twisted iron with flattened ends. They were often used in bundles of twenty; two hundred bundles could comprise the bride-price. At the end of the nineteenth century, ten oranges or ten bananas could sell for two Kissi pennies. In Liberia, among the Gbande tribe, when a man selects a wife, he first gathers a number of Kissi pennies. He then visits the home of the girl and, in the presence of the family, places a bundle of Kissi pennies on the girl's head and says, "This is my wife," as he hands over the first installment of his payments to her father.[2] It should be noted that in these three countries, Kissi pennies may constitute the essential part, or even the entire amount, of the bride-price. Another iron currency used in acquiring a wife is the imitation axe-head, in bundles of ten, called *bikei* or *ntet*. They are also called Fan axes. It was used by the Fan, Fang, and Mpongwe tribes of Gabon, and the Pangwe and Pahuin tribes in the Democratic Republic of Congo. It was the only currency used for bride-price there.

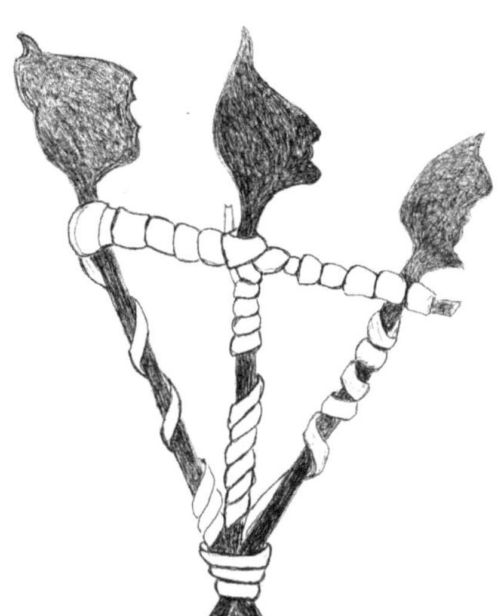

Fig. 44 Fan axes were only about five inches in length

Many iron items used in bride-price. The Ikonga spearhead was from the Democratic Republic of Congo and was another item used in bride-price, but could have also been useful for ceremonial purposes. It was made of cast iron. It had no shaft, because the wood deteriorated. In some tribal areas only the spearhead was considered the currency item.

The narrow hoe is also cast iron. This hoe money was used in central and northern Nigeria for various ceremonies, bride-price, and other large transactions.

Another cast iron piece is the idoma, which was plain looking, with a long tapered point that ended in a triangular shape. The idoma was used as a currency in Liberia, Nigeria, and the northern Democratic Republic of Congo. Its purpose was for bride-price and large transactions.

Another high-end currency was the marriage hoe found among the Madi tribe in the border area between southern Sudan and Uganda.

Fig. 45 In Sudan and Uganda, the marriage hoe was made solely for bride price.

The large Kwadja double hoe is made of forged iron by the Kwadja people in western Cameroon. Because of its size, it was important for bride-price, but could also purchase canoes. It probably served as a bullion source for smaller objects such as the Kissi penny. It was widely used also in northeastern Nigeria.

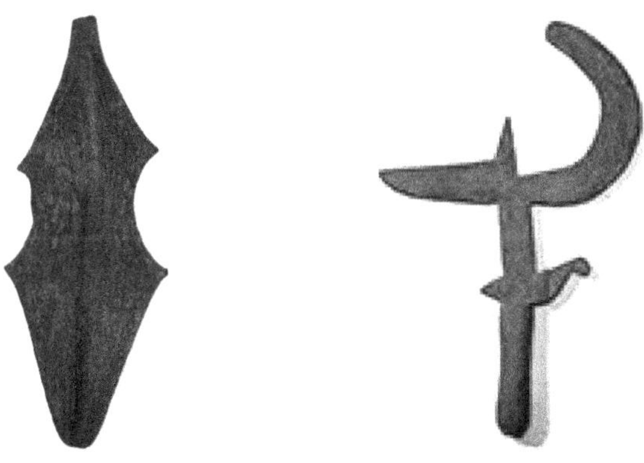

Above left: Fig. 46 The Kwadja double hoe. Right: Fig. 47 The Ngombe throwing knife was made of forged iron and was seldom used as a weapon.

The Ngombe throwing knife was used by the Ngombe, Lingombe and Bagondo tribes in the Democratic Republic of Congo. Throwing knives were impractical to use for hunting in the forest areas of the Congo Basin. The knife was used as a tool, for ceremonies, as a bride price, as a currency for large transactions and as a symbol for ostentation. As a tool, it would be sharpened and used to cut trees down, clear brush and work the soil in preparation for farming. The ceremonial, display nature is not to be ignored.

The double gong is an interesting item. It was made by hammering out an iron bar into a sheet and then bringing the two edges together, forming a bell-like shape. This gong produces two notes that are a third apart on the musical scale. It was used for buying slaves, bride-price, and in official ceremonies. This gong was purchased in Kano, Nigeria, in 1975.

Fig 48 The double gong and the single gong were currency in many tribes from Togo to East Africa.

The purr-purr is a small hoe that was also cast iron money. It was important in larger transactions, bride-price, and for ceremonies. The round hoe is bowl shaped, with a small perpendicular tab. It also is cast iron. Found in the northern and central area of Nigeria, it was used for bride-price, larger transactions, and ceremonial purposes. The final cast-iron money item we'll look at is the spade hoe. It was used for bride-price and larger market transactions. The hoes were introduced briefly in chapter one. All of these iron pieces were not only legal tender; they were considered important keepsakes and often kept in the family for years as heirlooms. Families stored the items in the rafters of their hut for generations as special treasures.

Domestic slaves as a commodity. The second most important primitive money class, after iron, was slaves. Our Western society with its twenty-first-century mentality tends to look back at this and shake its collective head. Further, we like to think that the slavers captured these people and shipped them to foreign soil as the only destination. That is only a part of the slavery story, however. Slavery within Africa goes back many centuries. It is unsavory to think of slaves treated as a commodity, but they were just that. They were a store of value and a medium of exchange.

Fig. 49 This servant, slave woman was from Mogadishu, Somalia, in 1882.

Only very large transactions, including the negotiation of bride-price, involved slaves and cattle. In the Congo Basin in the 1920s, for example, a typical bride-price for a Basonge bride was "14 large crosses [Katanga], 1 large she-goat, 1 piece of indigo drill, 1 flint-lock gun and 1 female slave."[4] If there was some status in the family, two hundred goats, one hundred slaves, and three hundred crosses, as well as powder and shot, could be claimed. Because of the cumbersome nature of many of the items of primitive money, slaves were an important part of the transportation of this money. They sometimes transported the money and were themselves the money. Slavery will be dealt with more extensively in the next chapter.

Copper has "superior decorative value."[5] The next commodity we look at is copper, which was used in its pure form, and also alloyed with zinc to make brass. The Katanga cross was made of molten copper in the Katanga District in the southeastern part of the Democratic Republic of Congo, a region world famous for its copper production. Some crosses were several times the size and weight of this specimen, and some were just a few inches across.

Fig. 50 The Katanga cross was currency in many countries from Cape to Cairo; 6½" x 7½"

They also had the shape of a capital H. The casting mold was made by forming the shape with fingers in sand. In the 1920s the Katanga cross was often the basis for the bride-price payment. They were, in fact, made "at least from the middle of the 18th century to as late as the 1920s."[6]

Another form of copper currency widely used in the Congo Basin was the *boloko*. This was a very heavy gauge rod that had a croquet-hoop shape and was important in marriage payments. In the Olemba tribe, when a young man sought marriage, he would approach a girl and say, "I love you." If the girl was satisfied with this, she said, "All right, bring the money."[7] The payments then began. The boloko was also used in the purchase of slaves. A male slave might cost three to ten bolokos, while a female slave, of "guaranteed fecundity," might be two bolokos.[8]

Fig. 51 The boloko was a copper rod currency used in Democratic Republic of Congo

The twist and knot *bochie* is a copper bracelet made of "Calabar rod" currency. This rod was from the Calabar region of southern Nigeria. It began as a three-foot-long round bar, which was itself used as currency. The artisan split this bar into three equal three-foot strips and cleverly twisted them into a desired shape. A well-documented find of a buried brass bochie was dated to the twelfth century.

Fig. 52 The twist and knot bochie is an example of the early work of the copper artisans.

Legendary African fastidiousness. Manillas are crescent-shaped bracelets that were used as bride-price, as payments for fines, as payments for purchases in the local marketplace, and as a commodity in the slave trade. Manilla means "bracelet," and was one of the most common forms of money in Africa. However, there appears to be little evidence that this "bracelet" was ever utilized as a form of jewelry. There were nine different common or trade manillas, which were in use in various parts of Africa for centuries. These common manillas, produced in Europe, were the currency of the markets. The photograph in chapter one shows eight of those nine types of manillas.

In the port city of Calabar, in what is now Cross River State, Nigeria, in 1505 the Portuguese traders were pleased with the acceptance of this medium of exchange for slaves. When using them in a local market, however, the merchant would show no hesitation at all in refusing your manilla payment if it was not the "official" one in use in that market. It had to be "their" manilla, even though "the casual observer could scarcely distinguish between them, yet the practiced eye of the natives does it at once and is not deceived."[9] Eugenia W. Herbert tells of the legendary African fastidiousness where a buyer had gone through an entire barrel of manillas and accepted only one of them.[10]

There is beauty but also weight. The wave manilla from Chad and Nigeria is made of cast brass, and has a twisted, spiral body with an ornamented end. It is most attractive and is an interesting contrast to the common manillas. The Nupe tribe in the area of Bida, Nigeria, is noted for its crafts and lost-wax brass casting. Two white-brass Nupe bracelets are shown. The larger one has an eight-faceted body with thirteen enlarged facets at the ends. The smaller bracelet has a round body with thirteen faceted ends. Both have seen wear and are attractive, although all three bracelets are rather heavy.

Fig. 53 The wave manilla; an attractive cast brass currency we have little information on.

Fig. 54 The large Nupe bracelet is from the Nupe tribe in Bida, Nigeria.

Fig. 55 The medium Nupe bracelet is attractive, giving prestige to the one who owned it

Calico corners. Locally made native cloth was an essential part of marriage payments even into the 1940s in parts of Nigeria. The big item, though, in several sections of Africa in the early 1900s, was imported calico. The British brought it over, and it became an almost immediate hit. However, not all people of Africa admired it.

Fig. 56 On the huge African Plateau, calico was for some time the main medium of exchange.

Our story picks up in a remote village between the Loange and Kasai rivers in what was the old Belgian Congo (currently the DRC) in 1907. A trader brought in a generous stock of calico, which was the accepted currency in the surrounding area. There were no cloths of any kind in this village. However, the chief had issued an order that "any one of his subjects being found wearing European cloth would be instantly put to death."[11] This tended to have a negative effect on the sales of calico in that village. Not too far away from that village, in Northern Rhodesia (present-day Zambia) in 1910, calico was so popular that men were paid their wages in calico and were buried in calico, and it was often a part of the bride-price.[12] Both men and women used it to wrap around their lower bodies.

Bride-price, adultery, and murder. Mat money (also called raffia cloth and Kuba cloth) was very important at Loango, located on the Atlantic coast, in what used to be French Equatorial Africa, now Gabon. Mat money was woven of strips of raffia palm leaves. These strips were also made into sleeping mats. Whether the sleeping mats were one and the same as the currency mats is not known. The currency mats had a variety of sizes depending on the location where they were found, but the piece shown in the Data, Image and Citation Index is eighteen by sixteen inches. The Loango people called their pieces *madiba.* They sewed the pieces together in a configuration that was three pieces by ten pieces, so they had dimensions of six by fifteen feet. This they called *nta.* They were so fond of nta that it was used for fines, compensations, bride-price, and for money spent at funerals. The bride-price was an average of one hundred nta. If a wife took a lover, the husband claimed one hundred nta from his wife's lover. If a man murdered another man, he had to pay the relatives two hundred nta and a gun[13] as compensation. There seems to be no claim for the husband's lover.

Variable winds. In the Nupe Kingdom in western Nigeria, in 1942, cowrie shells were used as the payment for bride-price. Even though modern money was also available at that time, cowries were preferred.[14] The amount of money that was paid for the bride-price differed from tribe to tribe, from village to village, and from one era to another, and was dependent on the status of the groom as well as the status of the bride. It was an evolving process with variables indicating that it may be renegotiated in due time, as shown at the beginning of this chapter. Other variables included the level of education of both bride and groom, the relationship of either of them to the village chief, and the social standing of the two fathers in the village.

"The father vek *a wife . . ."* A few final thoughts on the subject of bride-price. Jane I. Guyer uses the term "bridewealth," which is described as the value placed on the potential bride in the marital agreement. The Beti tribe of Gabon uses the term *vek*, a verb meaning "to think, measure, or compare, and is used in the active tense in relation to marriage, as in 'The father vek a wife for his son.'" Note that nothing here implies that there is a sale, capture, or purchase. Instead, the notions surrounding this term suggest that there is an element of pondering and evaluating whether this male and this female are suitable for each other. Associated with this is the idea that the families of the bride and the groom are brought closer together. This is an important element for most tribes. Also important, it's true, is the monetary val-

ue. With the Beti, several steps are followed, the most important of which is the payment given to the father of the bride by the father of the groom. Most writers seem to dwell on only this last element.

An expensive wedding. There is an interesting example from the Beti tribe from the year 1960 of a very expensive vek. It begins with "69,000 CFA,* [about $350] in cash; 7 goats; 1 pig; 40 litres of red wine; 60 liters of palm wine; a case of beer; a carton of cigarettes; a carton of matches; 1 woolen blanket; 1 cotton wrapper; 4 other cloths; 7 dresses; 1 pair of shoes; 1 machete and a sharpening file; a tablecloth; and 4 glasses." It is true this is an expensive example. In contrast, today, 70 percent of the population of Gabon lives below the poverty line, living on less than $1.25 per day (about $465 per year). It should be noted in all of this that, in the event the marriage dissolved, all bride-price items had to be returned to the father of the groom. There is a story of a district magistrate from a city in the Congo Basin who arrived at his office one morning and found on his table some pieces of madiba (raffia cloth), a pair of suspenders, and a pile of Katanga crosses. He immediately recognized the situation: "Hello, a dowry returned. Another divorce."[15]

An app? You're joking! In Johannesburg, South Africa, a software developer has taken this long-standing African tradition of paying a

* CFA stands for Communauté Financière Africaine, or African Financial Community. One CFA franc equals ten centimes; there are two CFA systems, used by fourteen African countries.

Fig. 57 This cow with calf were part of the Nguni tribal lobola.

bride-price to a new level in the tech age. The developer, twenty-six-year-old Kopo Robert Matsaneng, has designed the Lobola Calculator, which will crank out the bride's value in rand, pounds, euros, or dollars. The app will then convert this into cows.

Lobola is the term South Africans use for the tradition of bride-price payment. Historically, lobola was paid in livestock. "The application considers the person's age, height, waist size, and how attractive they are: ranging from 'not at all' to 'really hot,'" *Bloomberg News* reported. Also considered is whether she has a job, if this is a first marriage, and whether she has children. Reporter Franz Wild noted: "While most users liked the app, some objected that it was not in tune with the true value of lobola." Additionally, the app gives averages for other countries in southern Africa. The highest value was 100,000 rand ($8,757), or twelve cows, while the lowest was 35,000 rand ($3,065), or five cows.

The South African Minister of Home Affairs announced on November 21, 2016, that he would introduce legislation to place strictures on the practice of lobola. Under the new law, men would be able to demand a refund of the lobola if they were unhappy in their relationship with their wives. At time of writing, there is no final word yet from South Africa, but a good amount of discussion is ongoing in the media.

We in the West can look at the notion of bride-price and smile, but it was, and still is, a very important institution in many African countries. It is apparent that "bride-price" has evolved somewhat on the African continent. However, it still brings two families together in a negotiated financial arrangement.

CHAPTER FIVE

Money and the Merchants

"Saving and investment is very difficult in a barter economy."
—ALAN GREENSPAN, former chairman of the Federal Reserve Board

Travel by compass, stars, or cairns. A merchant is one who trades in commodities produced by other people in order to earn a profit. The merchants involved in our context are additionally concerned with commercial transport of goods over distances of a few hundred miles to thousands of miles. The mode of travel might have been by camel (introduced to Africa in the first century B.C.),[1] by foot, by donkey, or by boat. The geographical conditions included the desert with no roads, the Sahel (the semiarid region between the Sahara Desert and the savannah), the savannah, and the tropics. Though the compass was probably introduced in the region in the 1300s, navigation was primarily by the stars and by landmarks such as buttes, trees, rocks, cairns, and mountains. (A cairn is a mound of rocks that is built specifically as a landmark.) Caravans have used all of these guides for thousands of years. The commodities traded included salt, gin, slaves, trade beads from Europe, calico from Great Britain and later from India, cowrie shells from the Maldive Islands off the coast of India, and manillas and raw materials from several European countries. Salt, gin and slaves will be our concern in this chapter.

Salt. The oldest evidence that we have of salt processing goes back eight thousand years to what we now call Bulgaria.[2] Wherever salt is found, it is either processed from salt mines or evaporated from sea water or mineral-rich spring water. Salt is important to all human beings because it is essential to our health and because it is one of the five basic taste sensations. Stories from traders, explorers, and missionaries show that this craving for salt was no small matter, and included the idea of exchanging "gold for an equal weight of salt."[3]

A special contact. Salt was one of the longest serving and most important monetary commodities in Africa during the primitive money era. A. Hingston Quiggin, writing about the Congo, relates an interesting story dealing with salt: "The natives are so fond of the taste that successive possessors of this money can rarely resist a lick. Hence, after serving for several transactions it reaches the final consumer sticky with saliva, and thick with dirt, which happily does not affect the stomach of the negro."[4] (This is not the time to introduce the concept of laundered money. However, the following is a contrasting account to accompany this unhygienic tale.)

May your salt ring true. In 1899, the British explorer Major Powell Cotton was traveling in the capital of an unnamed African country. He found salt bars there in four different denominations, with values of one-and-a-half, one, a half, and a quarter Maria Theresa thalers. He was using the small bar (ten inches long, two inches wide) as his small change. It was four to the thaler. In attempting to change a thaler into salt bars, he found it "was not the work of a moment; each bar had to be examined and sounded, for if it were not of the right size, was chipped or cracked or it did not ring true, the first person to whom it was offered would be as indignant as a London cabby when tendered a bad shilling."[5] No salt licks here!

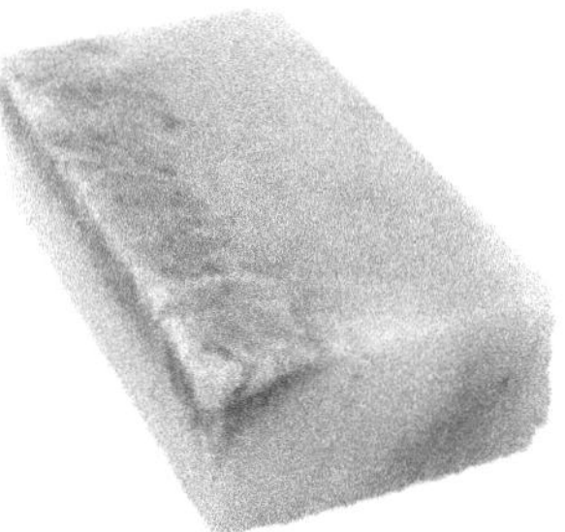

Fig. 58 Salt bars in Katanga, Democratic Republic of Congo, came in 6½ lb. size.

"You are the salt of the earth."[6] Taghaza is an old, unattractive salt-mining town that was abandoned in the late sixteenth century. It was located in what is now the northwest corner of Mali, close to the Tropic of Cancer. The only residents of Taghaza were slaves of the Masufa, a Berber tribe, who lived in houses made from slabs of salt with camel skin for a roof. Their mosques were built of the same mate-

rial. Ibn Battuta, the Moroccan geographer, explorer, and scholar who traveled Asia and Africa for thirty years, passed through this region in 1352, stating that "the water was brackish and the place is plagued with flies."[7] The caravan he was traveling with stayed there in discomfort for ten days. There were no trees or plant life there: it was nothing but sand and salt. He saw how they chiseled the salt from the pits and placed one gigantic slab on each side of a camel for transport to the Sudan.

His caravan, however, was not a salt caravan; he was simply on his way to the Sudan.

Fig. 59 This camel will walk forty miles per day and does not need food or water for one week.

Travel problems. If we were to stop at this juncture and review the situation of Ibn Battuta, we would find some remarkable details. He was going to store a ten-day supply of the brackish Taghaza water for his journey: it would take them a minimum of ten days to get to the next watering hole. He found one dead body on the way, only one mile away from water. He had begun to cross the Sahara Desert, an area of 3,600,000 square miles, which is comparable to the size of the United States. Not only are there no roads; there are no paths to follow. The sands are constantly shifting. They have the landmarks, stars and a compass. There is virtually no cloud cover and the average high temperature is 100.4° to 104.0° F. As if this were not enough: "The guide whom we had was blind in one eye and diseased in the other, yet he had the best knowledge of the road of any man."[8] (The eyesight comment sounds like the opening line of a barroom joke. There must be some humor also in the reference to a "knowledge of the road.") Four and a half centuries later, in 1805, a salt caravan along the same Timbuktu–Taghaza route, with 2,000 men and 1,800 camels, perished while heading home to Timbuktu—"not a man or beast being saved."[9]

Fig. 60 A salt caravan crossing the Sahara Desert may include hundreds or even thousands of camels.

"Mankind can live without gold but not without salt." In Taghaza, "the salt trade was on a grand scale, with caravans of hundreds of camels all laden with salt. And it 'passed for money' wherever it went."[10] Salt, as a commodity in much of Africa, was a medium of exchange and was also a standard of value in some places. It set the standard by which all items in a local market were valued. In Luluaberg in the Congo Basin, in 1924, the women road workers were paid by the bucketful of salt, and spent it in the local market by the teaspoonful. Salt was available in bars, cubes like sugar cubes, and crystals. When the bars were broken up into halves and quarters, the divisions were remarkably accurate even when done as the need arose.

Safety on the "road." When these caravans got underway from the salt mines, a reasonable security force accompanied them. The valuable cargo had to be protected. During that era, all travelers were careful to wait for a caravan that was passing close to their destination. The problems they faced included getting lost, running out of water, and vandals. One reference from the 1850s describes a caravan of 3,800 camels.[11] A rough estimate of the value of this cargo was eight thousand pounds sterling. You can be assured that protection was important!

* Cassiodorus, a sixth-century Roman statesman and writer.

*"When it rains it pours."** Another productive mine during this era was in Ethiopia. Alexander Hamilton, a merchant from India, wrote in the eighteenth century: "The current small money of Ethiopia is salt, which is dug out of the mountains as we do Stones from our Quarries, which they break into Pieces of several sizes, the largest weighing about 80 pounds, the others in 40, 20, 10, or 5 pounds."[12] The value of the twenty-pounder was one British shilling. As in the case of Taghaza, camel caravans departed from the mines in different directions. Besides the mines, people in several locations produced the salt crystals from evaporated seawater or salty spring water. One of these areas was in the Basanga District of Zambia. The salt was produced by filling baskets with the saline earth, then pouring water through it. The salty water was then left to evaporate. Finally, the salt crystals were placed into baskets one foot long and three inches wide. The salt baskets were then a form of currency: "5 of them were equal to a male calf, 3 were equal to a suckling calf and 20 to a heifer."[13]

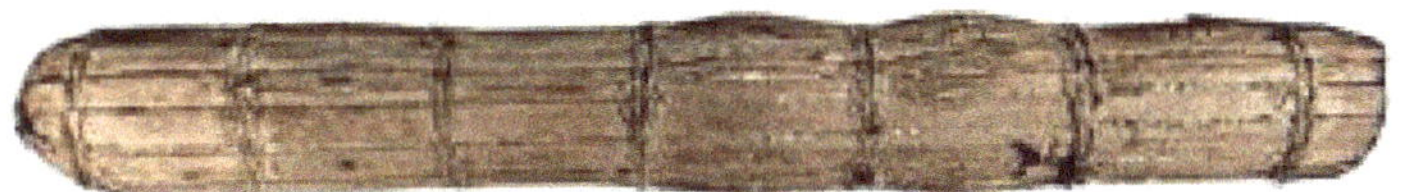

Fig. 61. Packaged salt in crystal form.

---

* This is the motto, since 1914, of Morton Salt, an American food company.

To consume or not to consume. Another commodity that the merchant was concerned with was gin, which served as a medium of exchange and a store of value. Gin was a prominent currency in eastern and central Nigeria, and in a smaller section of northern Nigeria. Gin was introduced to Nigeria when a few tribes smuggled it in from neighboring countries, and it soon became a form of investment for tribal chiefs. Unlike perishable foodstuffs, this commodity could pass from hand to hand for several years without going bad. Paul Einzig writes: "Gin and rum, too, served as a means of payment with the usual destructive effect on the physique and morals of the natives."[14] Gin was used in bride-price by the Yoruba and the Ekoi tribes and also served as a commercial currency.

Fig. 62 Bottles of gin were a commodity in Nigeria, DRC, and also in trade with Europeans.

"At the end of the 19th century a bottle of gin was worth 5 manillas,"[15] while in 1905 a crate of twelve bottles was forty brass rods or fifteen shillings in Cross River area in southeast Nigeria. It became a very popular currency in several areas of Nigeria. One reason for its popularity was that its value was often on the rise. This occurred because of increases in the duty the government imposed on all imported spirits. The demise of gin as a currency occurred several years later, with the outbreak of the First World War. In 1914 the Nigerian government forbade all importation of spirits, and at that point gin ceased to circulate as a currency. As Sven-Olof Johansson commented, "What happened to it then is perhaps not too difficult to guess."[16]

Forms of slavery in Africa. Slavery in Africa took many forms: there were domestic helpers who worked for someone in exchange for food and shelter, those who sold themselves or their child in order to pay a debt, those who were captured in wartime and were in servitude to their captors, those who were recruited (often deceitfully) or kidnapped as sex slaves, and those who were purchased as commodities on the open market. When the term *slave* is mentioned, most readers think of the chattel slave that was common in the United States, but whatever form of slave is being considered, there are some issues in common. The rights and privileges granted by the master were important. That would include whether the slave may marry, own property, or even buy their way out of slavery. The issue here is whether the slave was granted any "free will" and just what kind of relationship there was with the master.

The chattel slave. The chattel slave was treated as personal property and bought and sold for domestic use, or was exported as part of the

Atlantic trade. In all of the forms mentioned, the owner or master may have shown a humanitarian understanding and a compassionate attitude toward his property. In the mid-fourteenth century Ibn Battuta was visiting the kingdom of Mali and was given a slave boy as a "hospitality gift." This favorable-appearing act was not always the case, however, and there are many references to the opposite extreme, especially with the Muslim slave traders. Some traders did not know the word compassion, and the survival rate for slaves was very low from home village to the auction platform in the port of entry.

Unmentioned so far is the slave that was used as human sacrifice. There do not appear to be a large number of areas where this was practiced, but where it was accepted, a special caste of slaves was used.

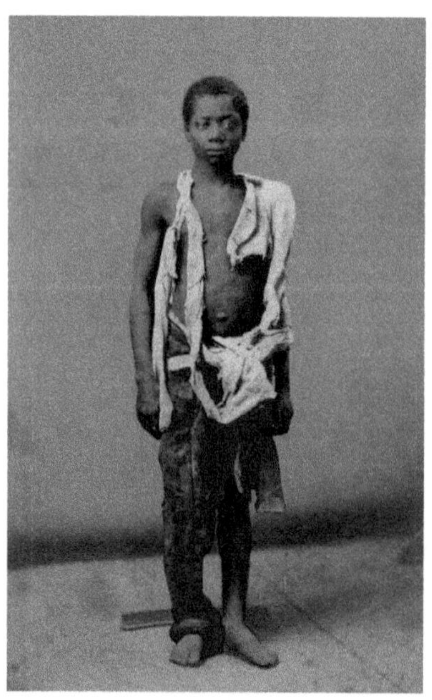

Fig. 63 Slavery for this Yoruba boy and all of humankind is now outlawed in all countries of the world.

Hard facts. The worldwide attitude, both pro-slavery and anti-slavery, during the primitive money era was shaped by the following facts:

- Slavery existed before the time of written history.

- The Bible recognizes the existence of slavery: Leviticus 25:44–46, Exodus 21:7–11, I Peter 2:18, Ephesians 6:5–8.

- In 1444 Portugal brought the first 235 African slaves from Mauritania.

- In 1452 Pope Nicholas V issued a papal bull allowing Portugal to enslave "pagans."*

- In the 1450s Portugal introduced horses into Africa; one horse purchased fifteen slaves.

- In 1505 the Portuguese purchased slaves in Calabar, Nigeria, for eight to ten manillas each.

- In 1800 more than half the populations of South Carolina, Maryland, and Virginia were slaves.

- One in four slave ships failed to reach their home port due to storms, rebellion, or capture.

- In 1809 a high of $40,000 (adjusted to 2018 dollars) was paid for a slave in the U.S.

- The average journey across the Atlantic Ocean lasted two months.

- A total of 380,000 slaves were sent to Southern cotton fields in the U.S.

---

* A papal bull is a public decree issued by the pope of the Roman Catholic Church to all its members.

- A total of 10.7 million slaves survived the journey across the Atlantic Ocean (85.6 percent of those that started the journey).

- From 1526 to 1867, 12.5 million slaves were shipped to the Americas from Africa.

- Slavery still exists in Mauritania, with 150,000 slaves out of a population of 3.8 million.

Fig. 64 Mary Slessor came to Nigeria as a twenty-eight-year-old and stayed for thirty-nine years.

Mary Slessor, missionary extraordinaire. With all of that background, we now shift to an unusual missionary story dealing with a slave. Mary Slessor was born on December 2, 1848, in Aberdeen, Scotland, of an alcoholic father and a devout Christian mother. She was raised in Dundee, Scotland, in an impoverished setting during the Industrial Revolution. At the age of fourteen, she rose to the skilled position of a weaver, working a full shift, followed by six hours in school.

In 1876, at age twenty-eight, Mary was accepted as a missionary to Nigeria, and after three months of training, departed on August 5 of that year. After a five-month journey, she arrived in Duke Town, just outside of Calabar, in what is now Cross River State, Nigeria. Her challenges began in earnest when she arrived. She had to learn the Efik language and traditions. Those traditions included the prevalent superstitions and witchcraft. There were also tropical diseases to learn about, and aggression from some local tribes to cope with. But learn and cope she did. By the time she passed away on January 13, 1915, she had built several mission stations that included schools and churches. "Her teaching, caring and nursing skills, and ability to sort out local disputes in a just manner, made her much more than a missionary."[17] What the people of the Calabar area will remember her for mostly will be her rescue of abandoned children, her improvement of the lives of women, and especially her work in eradicating the murder of twins that was so common there. All three of these acts were related to her deep reverence for life.

"We've some very peculiar customs down here regarding twins."[18] This comment was made by an Englishman to a newcomer to the continent. In much of western Africa there was a sense of the surreal and unnatural whenever twins are born. Some of the customs were more eerie and unsettling than others. For instance, the Akele of southeastern Nigeria had the tradition of restricting the mother to her hut for one year after giving birth to twins. This was followed by a traditional ceremony, after which she was allowed to resume her normal activity.

Before Miss Slessor's arrival, twins in the area where she worked were immediately killed upon birth. The reasoning was that one of the twins was the offspring of the devil because the mother must have mated with the devil. Further, it being impossible to determine which twin was the devil's, they were both killed. Tragically, in this area the mother was also killed because of her perceived involvement with the devil.

Among the Tschwi of West Africa, when one of the twins died, the surviving twin was given a fetish doll to hold on to. They believed the doll was inhabited by the deceased twin's soul. The idea was that they did not want that soul to feel lonely and wander about and take the living twin away with it. The terror and fear with which twins were regarded in the many tribes of southeastern Nigeria is mysterious and unsettling, but at the same time very real.

Fig. 65 Two wooden fetish dolls that were very crudely made and painted.

Coming to a theater near you. This next Mary Slessor story is about an Ibo slave who was owned by a "big woman" in a tribe and who treated the slave with great kindness and consideration. The young slave was never named in the citation, so we'll call her Miss X. Miss X became pregnant, and on the arrival of a pair of twins in her hut, there was an abrupt change in the relationship that everyone had with her. An entirely different set of rules entered the situation. Immediately she was subjected to virulent abuse by her owner and the village. A beautiful set of English china basins, which she valued highly, were smashed and broken, and her clothes were torn up. With great emotion and high drama, she was driven off the compound as an "unclean" being, similar to a leper. At this point it was time for the village to take over. If Miss Slessor had not been in the area, and the fear of her deep anger concerning this superstition, Miss X and her twins would have been killed at this juncture, and their bodies cut up and thrown into the bush a long way from the footpath. In the eyes of rural Nigerians, a footpath is supremely important: it is their communication link; it is their transportation connector; it is their public access to the next village. In their eyes, this precious conduit was now being contaminated by this lowly creature, limping slowly along with all of her possessions on top of her head.

Shifting scenes. Miss Slessor had heard of the twins' arrival. Departing from her isolated house with a bare head and bare feet, she headed immediately for the footpath that Miss X would likely be on. After four miles, she saw the woman coming toward her with the howling villagers behind her. Here was Miss X limping along, carrying a gin case containing her twins on her head, and on top of that a big brass skillet, and then her two market calabashes. (I cannot imagine that the twins were asleep during all of this commotion. We have to imagine the two sets of lungs getting practice.)

Miss Slessor to the rescue! She immediately took charge, relieving the weak, staggering woman of her load. What happened next is unusual. They waited while Miss Slessor's men cut a fresh path with their machetes to her home through the undergrowth, in the broiling heat, at the height of the hot season. In the eyes of the villagers, the path that Miss X had taken was so thoroughly polluted that it would have to be replaced. It was the important market path that Miss Slessor was trying carefully to save. They finally arrived, by way of the new path through the heavily wooded area, at Miss Slessor's home, where a modicum of order could be reached without the howling mob and the pressure of the disastrous traditions.[19]

The conclusion of this tale is interesting. The twins, a boy and a girl, were crammed into a gin case with such force that the boy's head was crushed. He died of the injuries and was given a burial at the proper time. The girl was left at Miss Slessor's growing orphanage, and the mother was able to return to her position with the "big woman" on the condition that there were no children.

Fig. 66 The author found Mary Slessor's tombstone in Calabar, Cross River, Nigeria.

Primitive money. It may appear, at first reading, that the entire section about Miss Slessor in the Cross River area of Nigeria made no mention of money in any form. However, be reminded that in this story a slave was involved and slaves were money. In many parts of Africa, recall that slaves were the second most important commodity in use. Miss X even happened to be an Ibo slave, who were considered more valuable than most other slaves.

The great demise. There is one final point to be clarified regarding the existence of slaves as a commodity in Nigeria and in Africa. Sir Alan Burns helps us out here: "There are three principle reasons for the existing [*sic*] of slavery in Nigeria, namely the total absence of free labour, the practical absence of coin currency and the need for a convenient form of transport."[20] There is a link between this "convenient form of transport," Mary Slessor with the slave Miss X, and the demise of primitive money in Nigeria and in Africa. At the same time as the tale of Mary Slessor with Miss X was unfolding, primitive money was falling out of favor in Nigeria. This demise was being aided by a lack of slaves to transport the currency. The slaves were the vehicle by which money was moved from point A to point B, and if they were not available it would affect the movement of money. "With the end of slavery, the other primitive forms of currency also lost their importance since they could not be carried for any great distance except by means of slaves."[21]

CHAPTER SIX

Money and Metallurgy

"I wasn't worth a cent two years ago, and now I owe two million dollars." —Overheard by MARK TWAIN

The smith and the smelter. The smith and the smelter held very respected positions in most villages. They may have been despised or disliked, but they were still feared and revered above all other mortals. They were regarded as priests, artists, shamans, or even magicians. In *Red Gold of Africa*, Eugenia W. Herbert writes: "The smith plays a central and powerful role in both the natural and the supernatural spheres."[1] The villagers believed these mystical men entered into the very bowels of the earth to extract the ores, and even competed with the gods. They were not to be trifled with.

Definitions. To appreciate the processes that were used to produce the primitive money artifacts, we must start by defining some terms. Metallurgy, defined loosely, is the technical science that looks at the properties of metals, and determines how to purify the metals and how to produce useful items from them. The following definitions are from *Pride of Men: A Glossary of Technical Terms* by Colleen E. Kriger:

1. *anneal:* to subject metal to a process of alternately heating and slow cooling in order to toughen, reduce brittleness, and improve elasticity; it is tempered. Copper requires a few hundred degrees C (200° Celsius = 392° Fahrenheit).

2. *anvil:* a solid mass of stone or metal, shaped with a working surface suitable for hammering out metal into objects.

3. *bellows:* an instrument designed to pump or force air into a fire or furnace.

4. *bloom:* the heterogeneous mass or chunks of iron metal produced by an iron smelt, particularly at the stage before refining out most unwanted impurities such as slag and charcoal.

5. *bowl furnace:* a type of smelting furnace made by digging out a curved hole in the ground.

6. *cast iron:* iron that has reached liquid form by melting, and is then poured into a mold; cast iron has a carbon content of about 2–4.5 percent.

7. *forge:* a fireplace where a blacksmith (smith) works metals by heating and hammering.

8. *foundry:* a workplace where furnaces operate to smelt ore and/or where metals are melted and poured into molds to make ingots or cast artifacts.

9. *hematite:* a mineral ore of reddish color; the major source for smelting iron ore into iron metal.

10. *ingot:* a block of metal, for example iron or copper, that is typically oblong in shape.

11. *laterite:* a reddish soil found in the tropics, often with sufficient mineral content to be used as an ore for smelting (e.g., iron, manganese, aluminum).

12. *shaft furnace:* a type of furnace design that includes some form of vertical structure or walls, sometimes placed over a pit or hole in the ground.

13. *slag:* waste materials that have melted and flowed out of mineral ore during a smelt.

14. *smithing:* working metal when it is hot and malleable by hammering it. It is referred to as forging the metal.

15. *smelt:* to melt or fuse an ore, thereby separating the metallic constituents. Copper requires 1,083° C (1,981° F).

16. *steel:* a term often used to refer to iron that is tougher and harder than wrought iron; it has a carbon content between cast iron and wrought iron: .25–1.75 percent.

17. *wire-drawing:* a copper ingot is first hammered into a rod and then

with pincers and droplet made smaller and smaller.

18. *wrought iron:* a term used to refer to alloys of iron and carbon that are soft and malleable, with carbon content less than 0.15 percent and impurities less than 1 percent.

Iron processes. Several processes and procedures were followed in order to create a finished product. In precolonial Africa two kinds of furnaces were used: the shaft furnace and the bowl furnace. These would be in contrast to the blast furnace in use in Europe at the time. Some African metallurgists hollowed out large termite mounds to use as a shaft furnace.

Fig. 67 One set of bellows for this open bowl furnace.

As well as a furnace, a metallurgist needs fuel, ore, and energy. The fuel was generally charcoal, made from a hardwood that burned slowly. If necessary, wood chips were used to supplement the charcoal. Mining the ore required specialized workers. They would clean the ore, crush it, and form it into small balls, ready to be fed into the furnace. The goal was to produce a bloom using the natural flow of air or by using the air supplied by the hand-operated bellows. The time span for the smelt could be as long as a month. (Imagine tending an operation for twenty-four hours a day, seven days a week, for four long weeks!) Once the bloom was formed, it had to be further refined by removing the slag and impurities. This was now the smith's role; using his forge, he hammered and heated the material, repeating the process again and again. His goal in the repetition was to remove as much of the impurities as he could.

Fig. 68 This bowl furnace has two sets of double bellows; note delivery of charcoal and ore.

Fig. 69 Shaft furnace with a natural draft; note the numerous workers feeding fuel and ore.

Production problems. Processing iron and copper ore in the tropics was a highly specialized art. The smith and the smelter went through a long internship. Yet there were many principles that they were not aware of. The design of their furnaces had much bearing upon the efficiency in producing a bloom. One production problem related to the use of low-grade ores. Again, the quality was affected, for higher grade ore produced more iron at higher standards. Next was the issue of the season during which they worked. If you cannot control the weather, you have to cooperate with it: both the mining and the smelting occurred during the dry season. Humidity as well as rain were problematic. The moisture in the air affected the charcoal burning as well as the moisture content in the hand-formed balls of crushed ore.[2] (Note all of the risky variables present in the description of iron production where the goal may have been to form objects of primitive money. This is a sharp contrast to the U.S. Mint with its controlled conditions, producing 27,900,000 pennies in one day.)

Operations with complications. Of all of the hundreds of forges and furnaces that existed in Africa in the precolonial period, there were many adaptations of the processes just mentioned. There are even examples where the numerous specialties were all done by the same smith and smelter. In general, however, the following is true: "Ironworking consists of a number of separate operations: mining, preparing the ore, manufacturing charcoal or other fuels, constructing the smelting furnace, smelting proper, refining or otherwise treating bloomer iron for forging, and finally smithing the finished objects."[3]

Copper processes. To process copper ore was likewise no simple matter in precolonial times (or today). It was a technically complex process, requiring a large amount of ore and a large amount of fuel. The smelt required such a high temperature that it could take a good long day or up to several days. Once the smelt was started there was no turning back; it was an ongoing process. The air intake and the fuel supply had to be maintained during that time.

The supernatural ritual and its prohibitions. Before any smelting or refining could begin, an initial ritual had to occur. Eugenia W. Herbert tells us about the master smelter, who was referred to as the "*maître sorcier*" ("master sorcerer") or the *nganga*. He was present at all of the crucial stages in the metalworking processes, collaborating with his fellow smiths. Before a mining operation began in the Katanga mine in the Democratic Republic of Congo, he invoked his predecessors and mentors to propitiate the spirits of the mine: "You who have preceded us, it is you who have opened for your children the entrails of the mountain. Grant that we may find treasure." He drove three stakes into the soil where shafts would be located in order to give protection against cave-ins, and then spat on the ground. The spit contained a concoction of bark to speed the discovery of the veins of copper ore.[4]

A mud bath. East of Katanga, in the Luishia area of the Democratic Republic of Congo, the nganga, or master smelter, arrived before the miners and would build fires around the periphery of the mine. He would then distribute green leaves on the fires in order to purify the mine of any evil spirits. In the evening he would take some cinders from the fires and distribute them in mine pits. Next, he would take some of the same cinders, certain roots, and a pinch of powered ore, and mix them all together with water. This concoction was then rubbed on the entire bodies of each miner in the morning at the worksite. In some mining areas, the charcoal preparation was also ritu-alized. At smelter sites, lighting the charcoal was preceded by a ritual, and there was a separate ritual for starting the bellows.

Sexual overtones. In the region of Kayes in western Mali, a large two-hundred-pound bloom was dragged from the furnace still steaming, and water was poured on it. The women from town came forward and lifted their skirts in order to absorb the vapors. Others collected the water that ran off from the cooling process and drank it. They all had to absorb the *nyama*, the vital force from the bloom. There is a further female fertility analogy with the "female furnace." Two protrusions sticking out from the body of the furnace represented breasts. At Law-ra, in northern Ghana, women who'd had stillborn babies were per-mitted to come to the smelting furnace in order to deliver their next babies so that that they may be born strong. A child thus born was called "*sabo*," that is, one born by the forge.[5]

All bases covered. In order to further prevent the failure of a smelt, several prohibitions were in force. No women or children were al-lowed within view of certain stages of the smelting process, especially at the smelting furnace site itself (except as noted above). No worker was allowed to have sexual relations with a woman the day preceding the beginning of a smelt. Lastly, no man was allowed to have any con-tact with a menstruating woman prior to a smelt. By keeping women

away from the furnace site, the smelter was able to more easily main-
tain control over the knowledge and expertise he possessed. May it be
noted here that all of the rituals and the prohibitions provided a ready
excuse in the event that a smelt did not go well!

CHAPTER SEVEN

Money Models

"Money is like manure. Stack it up and it stinks. Spread it around and it makes things grow." —ANONYMOUS

Beauty, balance, and grace in design. The word *model*, as used in the chapter title, has the definition "noun: a particular design or version of a product."[1] Some of the primitive money items are models of farming tools, hunting implements, status symbols, bracelets, and body decorations. However, there are many other items where it is not clear at all just what motivated the design. The Kissi penny may be modeled after the *sombe* penny, but what inspired that design? We can only speculate on what inspired the grooved rod with the flattened ends. It was, though, a very important currency to those living in Guinea, Liberia, and Sierra Leone.

Above left: Fig. 70 Kissi pennies, the "currency with a soul."
Right: Fig. 71 The sombe penny came before the Kissi in Sierra Leone, Liberia and Guinea.

Aside from this matter, you may have noticed that the definition we are using says nothing concerning the aesthetic nature of the item. Beauty, balance, and grace are evident in many of the money items, whether fashioned from brass, bronze, copper, iron, tin, shell or fabric.

Several of the throwing knives are good examples. The two that are shown are the *trombash* and the Mangbetu throwing knife. Their primary purpose was to indicate the owner's power and position of authority. The design of these knives evolved from the weapons, "but were gradually transformed into idealized symbols."* They did evolve then, as a currency.

* As stated by Tom Joyce in *Life Force at the Anvil*, p. 15.

On this and the following pages are miscellaneous examples of primitive money showing an artistic nature.

Above left to right: Fig. 72 narrow hoe; fig. 73 Mbole hollow legband; fig. 74 liganda.

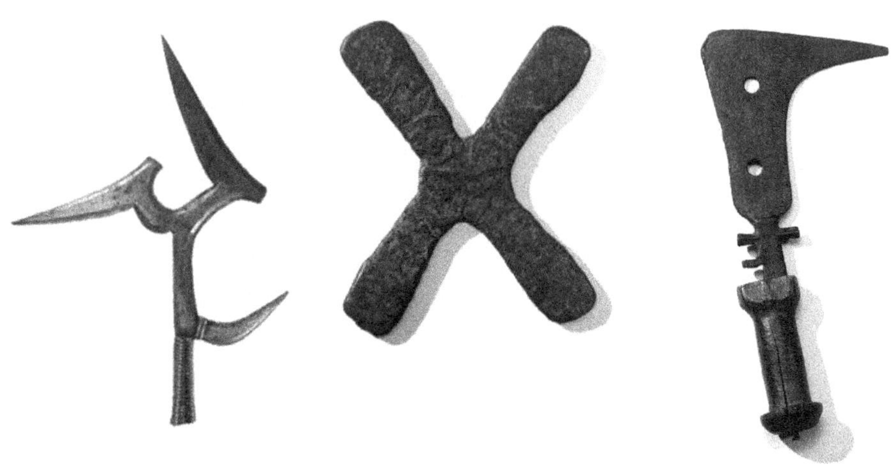

Above left to right: Fig. 75 Bwaka throwing knife; fig. 76 Katanga cross; fig. 77 trombash throwing knife.

Above left to right: Fig. 78. Congo leg band; fig. 79 boloko; fig. 80 Nupe bracelet.

Above left: Fig. 81 Kwadja double hoe; top right: fig. 82 Senufo boat anklets; bottom right: fig. 83 minkata.

Above left to right: Fig. 84 double gong; fig. 85 Idoma; fig. 86 konga leg band.

Top left: Fig. 87 dubil; top right: fig. 88 raffia cloth; bottom: fig. 89 tajere.

The human body as a device for decorative display. What was it that motivated the wives, daughters, mothers, sisters, nieces, and female slaves of some wealthy man to wear these items of beauty and grace around their necks, arms, and legs, and in their hair? The female body from head to foot and to the tips of the fingers may be adorned with hair ornaments, earrings, necklaces, bracelets, collars, girdles, pendants, cache-sexes, anklets, bells, amulets, rings, and crowns. It should be clarified that some males also adorned themselves, but to a far lesser extent. Also, many of the items worn were not primitive money, but merely tasteful jewelry and clothing.

As to motivation, it may be difficult for some of us to remove ourselves from a Western twenty-first-century mindset and place ourselves in an African society that is several centuries old. However, as noted earlier, if we want to understand the people and what motivated them, we must attempt to understand their culture. The man of influence in the tribe or village was concerned with showing his accumulated wealth and his status within the village, in celebrating the mystique associated with copper and iron, and in demonstrating the power that he possessed as a result. When his kinfolk and employees wore these objects, both he and his people were elevated in status.

Just a passing fad, a few isolated instances, or a cultural phenomenon? Communication, transportation, and information technology in the eighteenth and nineteenth centuries were either nonexistent or undeveloped compared to today. The wearing of jewelry and currency items was a widespread phenomenon, and one that had been going on for centuries. In *Red Gold of Africa*, Eugenia W. Herbert writes: "Copper ornamentation is, or has been, quasi-universal in African societies. Scarcely a modern ethnographic survey or traveller's account from the past that is at all specific in describing jewelry does not mention such objects as worn by at least some fraction of a given population."[2] Copper was not the only material used; other texts mention brass, bronze, iron, ivory, fabric, and shells. Herbert includes accounts from across the continent. Some of the quotations are humorous, but also revealing:

"Their women weare a Ring of Copper about their Neckes, which weighted fifteen pound at least, about their armes little Rings of Copper that reach to their elbowes, about their middles a cloth of the Insandie Tree . . . on their legs Rings of Copper, that reach to the calves of their legs."[3] On the Mauritanian coast the blacks are unclothed but prizing beads, "brass bangles or like ornaments which they use in those parts."[4] On the northern Zimbabwe plateau where the people are "all naked, and only on their legs do the women wear some bracelets of copper."[5] The Nama ornamentation is evident in Namaqualand (located in present-day Namibia, Botswana, and South Africa), where "their dress consists of all kinds of beautifully prepared skins . . . gorgeously ornamented with copper beads . . . Their locks they thread with copper beads, covering their heads all over. Around their necks they have chains, slung round them 15 or 16 times. Many round copper plates suspended from these chains. On their arms they have chains of copper or iron beads which go round their bodies 30 or 40 times."[6]

Going big. After strings of beads that circle the body thirty or forty times, what's next? The answer is to "super-size" everything. Increase the weight and the massiveness. The French-American explorer and anthropologist Paul B. Du Chaillu claimed that the Mpongwe women in Uganda wore twenty-five to thirty pounds (11–13 kg) on each ankle.

Fig. 90 Women wearing konga leg bands.

Not far away, in the Middle Congo region, the Bangui preferred collars that weighed in at thirty-three to fifty-five pounds (15–25 kg). Explorer Camille-Aimé Coquilhat said, "In short, the well-turned woman of the world wears day and night a weight equal to the pack of a Belgian infantryman in the field."[7] What he meant by day and night is that the installation of this neckpiece was pretty much a permanent act. The woman went into the foundry or blacksmith shop and lay on the floor. The collar was fitted while resting on the anvil on the floor. Sometimes the collar was still warm and therefore more malleable. To remove this collar was no small matter. A wedge had to be placed in the open portion, forcing the two ends apart, once again while the woman lay on the anvil on the floor.

Diversity. If you look at the Data, Image, and Citation Index in the appendices, you will note a wide diversity in the color, design, physical size, weight, material, and method of development of primitive money. We have money examples from the animal kingdom, with cattle, goats, sheep, and camels. There are six examples of plant-based items: tobacco, *tukula*, raffia cloth (Kuba cloth, mat money), cloths, gin (mentioned in chapter five) and kola nuts. Tobacco currency was found in different forms—leaf, stick, twisted and coiled—and used in Zaria and Gombe Division, Nigeria, as well as in Angola, South Africa, and in several locations in East Africa. Two citations for tobacco were given by Mary Kingsley in Fan country in the Democratic Republic of

Congo, where she bought several pineapples for one tobacco leaf[7] and gave one of her Fan porters "tobacco to buy 'chop' with."[8]

Fig. 91 Tobacco in Angola in a coiled form reached about eight feet in length.

The Bushongo and Ubangi tribes in the Democratic Republic of Congo used tukula or camwood (*Baphia nitida*) after it was rotted, ground down, and formed into cakes as a currency. This tree was found along the coast from Equatorial Guinea to Sierra Leone.

Fig. 92 Tukula, as a currency, was often given as a gift, especially at funerals.

These currency cakes were one use, but the extract was also used in soaps, skin treatment, and red dye, while the wood itself was used in knife handles.

Kola nuts and conversation. In 1975, my teenage son and I visited the sculpture studio of a brass artisan in the historic Benin City, Nigeria. We were trying to take in as much as we possibly could of the ambience of the studio, and had many questions about the charming pieces for sale and the process that produced them. When another customer left and we were alone in the room, the artisan greeted us warmly. After we'd become better acquainted, he said, "If you are free this evening, why don't you return to the studio and we can eat kola nuts together and talk about cire perdue?" It was a memorable evening.[9]

Fig. 93. Kola nuts had a ceremonial, social, and currency function in Burkina Faso, Mali, and Senegal.

Cire perdue or lost-wax casting and primitive money. Was primitive money produced by the lost-wax process ever in use in Africa? I have found a number of sources, both online and in print form, as well as information from helpful colleagues, that indicate it was, though the answer is by no means definitive. The process of casting by way of the lost-wax method has been around for so many centuries that the possibility of finding a connection with primitive money is intriguing.

Details, details. Cire perdue means "lost wax" in French. The earliest examples date back to around 3700 BC, using the carbon 14 method of dating. The process began with the sculptor completing a work using wax as the medium. Beeswax was used at that time. The wax had to be soft enough to carve and mold, but hard enough to retain its shape. It allowed the sculptor to include very fine details. Next, a soft clay was placed around the entire sculpture, followed by a layer of firmer clay. This was baked in a kiln, thereby melting the wax. Much of the wax was lost unless an effort was made to recover it. When the wax had left the chamber through the prepared holes, molten brass was poured into the chamber. After cooling, the clay was removed from the sculpture, leaving a unique object. West African artisans evolved the process through multiple castings and by uniting two or more cast sections together. An advantage to this casting method over the ordinary open casting is that more intricate details are possible with the lost-wax process.

Was any African primitive money produced by the lost-wax process? After reading many books, visiting numerous online sites, and receiving replies from six present-day primitive money enthusiasts, I was unable to definitively answer this question. However, I came tantalizingly close. I tried to find as many examples as possible with citations indicating that the cast object was used as currency. It must be noted, however, that some of the citations I found were more credible than others. The closer they are to the era of primitive money, the better. After assiduous research, I turned up several examples linking lost-wax casting and primitive money.

1. Brass frog money from Cameroon. This was listed by Col. Phares O. Sigler in *Strange (Odd and Curious) Money of the World*, page 15; Charles J. Opitz in *An Ethnographic Study of Traditional Money*, page 14, and F. Morton Reed, *Odd and Curious . . .*, pages 58–59. However, none of the sources provided citations.

Fig. 94 This brass frog was made in Cameroon by the lost-wax casting process. Some question whether it was a currency.

2. Baoule anklet from the Ivory Coast. This was listed by Opitz, page 276, with no citations, and by Scott Semans, who listed it on his website under African Bracelet Money #176 with several citations: Opitz, Ballarini, and André Blandin. Blandin was very clear in his endorsement: "These heavy ornamental objects were made using the lost-wax casting technique and were used, in the past, as anklets thus witnessing the wealth of the woman and had a currency value for the payment of a dowry." This is a narrow definition but it does indicate a linkage. There is an additional listing of this same anklet on the website of an American gallery, though the tribe's name is spelled Baule. The listing notes: "These copper alloy forms, made by the lost-wax process, were recognized and used to store and transfer wealth." This gallery was, at the time, using a Canadian art consultant. No further citations are given. This does, however, suggest that the Baoule anklet was used as currency.

Fig. 95 The Baoule anklet was used to "transfer wealth," perhaps as a dowry-like item.

3. Bamun bracelet currency from Cameroon. This is another example from the same gallery. The listing notes: "These intricate copper alloy forms, made by the lost-wax process, were recognized and used as currency for rare but major purposes . . . Though often identified as a currency type it also served as a prestige object." There were two citations given from two books, but neither provided a link. The quotes were from the same Canadian art authority, writer, museum curator, and professor, now retired. I tried to contact him by different means and at different times over a period of a year and a half. When I finally reached him by phone he was evasive as to the connection of African primitive money and the lost-wax casting of the Bamun bracelet. His ambiguous and noncommittal response made it clear: there are no legitimate citations forthcoming and his quotations are to be ignored. Looking at the website recently, the long quote cited above has been removed from the site and the gallery owner has made a very appropriate statement of regret for previous claims.

Fig. 96 The Bamun bracelet is an excellent example of an intricate lost wax casting.

Fig. 97 A brass lost-wax casting of the Oba that was purchased by the author while visiting in Benin City, Nigeria.

Our hobby in action. In pursuit of this query, I contacted members of the International Primitive Money Society, and received six responses, excerpts of which are reproduced below.

1. "Lost wax cast seems quite intricate and labor intensive. Usually it is characteristic of money to be uniform from unit to unit, and low cost of production would seem important also, so would think a reusable mold would tend to indicate items made as money while lost wax would tend to place items in the category of art objects—not that these are mutually exclusive, but would tend to be."

2. "We [Europeans] know of no African currencies produced by the lost wax method."

3. "While the Ashanti Gold Weights were not exactly a form of money, they seem to have been considered a valuable trade item and certainly were made by the lost wax casting process."

4. "Wax casting was widely used to manufacture brass and bronze gambling tokens during the Ayutthaya period (1351 to 1767) and also later in Siam [although it is not African]."

5. "If we approach the question properly we must define our terms. What money functions shall we demand; is just a medium of exchange adequate?"

6. "The very nature of lost-wax casting makes it unsuitable for the mass production of fungible items, so it is hard to see how it could be used to produce many currencies. However, the H-shaped copper ingots of central Africa may have been produced by lost-wax casting, and I have a gold one that may have been used for currency."

Conclusion: It ain't over till it's over. While there are tantalizing suggestions that lost-wax castings were used as currency, more research needs to be done. Comment five above is spot on. If we use a very loose definition for money, we might consider Ashanti gold weights as acceptable. Remember also that the barter system was present in many villages before, during, and after the primitive money era, and barter could easily be interpreted as currency use. For example, Henry M. Stanley and others may have had plenty of money, but they simply couldn't spend it in certain regions. Barter was the solution.

More validation is needed before we can offer a definitive answer to this intriguing question. Perhaps the work of a few obscure explorers, missionaries, or traders will someday be discovered that will help to make a more definitive conclusion.

CHAPTER EIGHT

Money and Mystique

"We just have to make sure the pockets are empty before we iron

the clothes." —An Australian discussing their plastic money

The medicine man. The definition that we shall use for *mystique* is: "a fascinating aura of mystery, awe, and power surrounding someone or something."[1] Mystery, awe, and power were associated with the witch doctor or medicine man, a prominent figure in the context of village life. He is called upon when illness occurs, when the outcome of a future event is desired, when a diviner is needed, and when an ancestral spirit must be contacted. Many villages had several medicine men, who often specialized. Some may diagnose illnesses and prescribe a cure and sacrifice, some may act as an oracle and predict future events, and some may deal in the black side of medicine such as casting curses. In general, they are the propagators of animism, the "belief in a super-power that organizes and brings the material universe to light."[2] It is that aspect of black magic that brings about fear, suspicion, and distrust from the villagers. When medicine men practice sorcery, cast spells, and deal in the occult, it is truly a dark art. At the same time, however, it must be recognized that "some perform good magic and are considered trustworthy."[3] Some have a reputation for curing illnesses and giving good council; they do not exploit the people, and are good tribal leaders in the village. These are an asset to their tribe and to their village.

Fig. 98 A medicine man dressed ceremonially for work with his noise-maker and much ornamentation, including beads, fetishes, and pouches.

White man no saby any ting. A story about the animism that many of the medicine men espoused comes out of Old Kalabar, on the coast of southeastern Nigeria, in 1858. The story is told by the British Consul for the Bight of Biafra and the Island of Fernando Po, who was visiting Old Kalabar. The people of that region believed that if any man killed a monkey or a crocodile, he would himself turn into a monkey or a crocodile when he died. The British-appointed governor tried to convince two local traders that this was nothing but "fool palaver," i.e., nonsense. He apparently got nowhere in the argument and was given a standard reply: "It be Kalabar 'fash' [fashion], and white man no saby any ting about it."[4] Translated: "You Europeans just don't understand us Africans." Sometimes these kinds of beliefs were locally or tribally oriented, and other times the acceptance was more widespread; in either case, they demonstrate the influence of animistic thinking.

The dark side. A further description of the animist influences may be helpful. During the eleventh century the Kingdom of Ghana had a large capital city, called Kumbi. It was divided into two parts. All of the Muslim residences with their twelve mosques were in one area; six miles away was an area called al-Ghaba, meaning "the forest." Located in al-Ghaba were the king's palace, the courts, the pagan or non-Muslim residences, the king's burial grounds, the center of the nation's spiritual life, and the prisons. No one was ever known to emerge from the prisons. Within the center of the spiritual life area were some groves or thickets where the fetish priests lived. This area was carefully guarded from intruders. The duty of the priests was to tend to the national gods and likely practice gruesome rites surrounding fetishism. The atmosphere in this setting is not a place where most people from the Western Hemisphere would feel comfortable at all.

The evil side. In Offa, southwestern Nigeria, in the early 1920s, a medicine man and his agents deliberately spread the smallpox virus to individuals who had not responded in a positive manner when threatened by them. They used blackmail to induce people to pay for protection from the virus. This deceitful side is explained to us by Langa Langa: "The most inoffensive individual would pay a heavy contribution to be enrolled as a member of the society—hoodwinked by the priesthood into the delusion that he would thus secure immunity from the disease."[5] Of course, there were further contributions for the privilege of retaining that membership. If someone did not cooperate, the agents would work the "juju" by jostling the victim in the marketplace or other large gathering place while sprinkling them with particles of dust or other infected matter collected from the body of someone stricken with smallpox. This was a highly effective way of terrifying the entire village. Most people were too terrified of the possible consequences to question the medicine man, although they were certainly fearful of him and his agents.

The wisdom of Solomon. The solution was a rather interesting one. The local people were too traumatized to accept any rational approach to the problem, so the representative of the British Governor-General's office was alerted when making his rounds. He was a young man, new in the country, but bold enough to jump into the conflict. He observed the process for a time, including numerous deaths, and slowly gained the confidence of several of the local leaders. Their cooperation followed only on the condition that he "would make a clean and impartial sweep of the priesthood and leave no offender at large to keep the worship alive."[6] In due time, he was able to imprison 12 of the ringleaders and caution 250 of the members and worshippers. He also set fire to three hundred fetishes (idols and charms). As the news spread, others in the village came and brought their symbols and charms and threw them into the burning fire. The following day, those from a neighboring village came and started a new fire on the same site that was larger than the original fire. A large sum of primitive money had changed hands during the course of this scandalous period through payments from blackmail and the exorbitant "contributions."

The medicine man and cupping. When a person was suffering from a disease, one form of therapy used by the medicine man was cupping. A level of heat was applied to the flesh and at the proper time a small bowl or cup was pressed onto the heated area and held there. The idea was to create a partial vacuum, and thereby draw the blood to the surface. At times fire was brought right to the surface of the skin, or a heated bowl or cup was placed on the surface of the skin. Whatever method was used, extreme heat was brought to the area. Used in nineteenth-century Africa, this therapy was likely lacking in the use of acceptable hygiene or even simple sanitation practice. Historians claim that the procedure goes back to 3000 BC, was practiced in Africa,

Asia, and the West, and was recommended by the Prophet Muhammad. Cupping remains widespread. It is practiced today in the West, though it is viewed by some as pseudoscience.

Fig. 99 A medicine man treating a diseased man through cupping.

Compensating the medicine man. How much money was paid for the services rendered by the medicine man was likely determined on a case-by-case basis. Perhaps the village chief was brought back to health after a moderate illness, or advice was sought by a man taking on a third wife, or a woman wanted a spell cast on a person who had stolen two of her chickens. In each case, the fee was calculated according to the services rendered, the person's ability to pay, whether it was the harvesting season, or even the standing of the medicine man in the community. A more difficult question to answer is what currency was used in the transaction. Any primitive money items in the local-market-purchase category could be used in payment. Whatever was useful on market day could be used to compensate the medicine man.

Primitive money items that might have been used as payment include Kissi or sombe pennies, cowrie shells, mat money (raffia cloth), manillas, and iron currency such as the purr-purr, various hoes, idoma, tajere, and the Katanga cross. An item not mentioned yet is the Togo stone money. It is a good candidate because it was a market-place currency. It was a two to two-and-a-half inch diameter white quartz disc shape with a hole in the center.

Fig. 100 Togo stone money was used in Ghana, Togo, and Sierra Leone.

Power gone astray. In Akim, a small village just next to Calabar, Cross River, Nigeria, was a "fetish man," or high priest, who was wealthy by mid-nineteenth-century standards. He was wealthy for good reason. In that area, when a man died and he had not adequately appeased the priest, the priest had the power to order that the corpse be placed in an upright position in the deceased's hut. If that upright position was retained, then the assets and property of the man remained with his family. However, if the corpse fell over, then all the effects of the deceased must be handed over immediately.[8] The medicine man was aware, of course, that the dead body was not likely to remain upright.

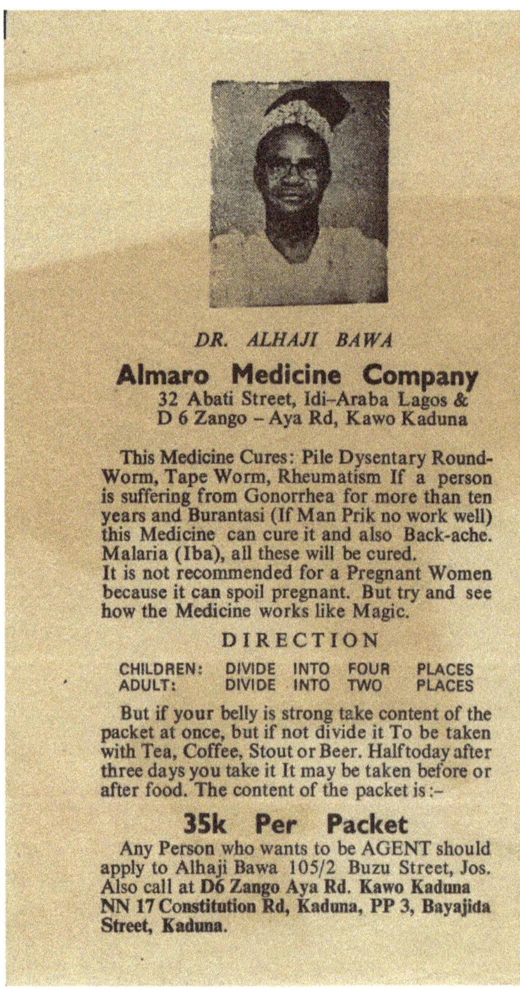

DR. ALHAJI BAWA

Almaro Medicine Company
32 Abati Street, Idi–Araba Lagos &
D 6 Zango – Aya Rd, Kawo Kaduna

This Medicine Cures: Pile Dysentary Round-Worm, Tape Worm, Rheumatism If a person is suffering from Gonorrhea for more than ten years and Burantasi (If Man Prik no work well) this Medicine can cure it and also Back-ache. Malaria (Iba), all these will be cured.
It is not recommended for a Pregnant Women because it can spoil pregnant. But try and see how the Medicine works like Magic.

DIRECTION

CHILDREN: DIVIDE INTO FOUR PLACES
ADULT: DIVIDE INTO TWO PLACES

But if your belly is strong take content of the packet at once, but if not divide it To be taken with Tea, Coffee, Stout or Beer. Halftoday after three days you take it It may be taken before or after food. The content of the packet is :–

35k Per Packet
Any Person who wants to be AGENT should apply to Alhaji Bawa 105/2 Buzu Street, Jos. Also call at **D6 Zango Aya Rd. Kawo Kaduna NN 17 Constitution Rd, Kaduna, PP 3, Bayajida Street, Kaduna.**

Fig. 101 The Almaro Medicine Company, Jos, Plateau State, Nigeria, 1974.

A 1974 Nigerian medicine man. In 1974, while shopping for food items in Jos, Plateau State, Nigeria, the small flyer shown above came to my attention. Dr. Alhaji Bawa made some very broad claims. First, no legitimate doctor in Nigeria in 1974 would have made those claims, so it is highly unlikely that he was a certified medical doctor. A medicine that could cure piles, dysentery, roundworm, tapeworm, rheumatism, gonorrhea, erectile dysfunction (*burantasi*), backache, and malaria would be a medical marvel. No prescription is needed, and you may take it with beer or stout. The cost was thirty-five kobo, equivalent to twenty-one cents (1974 USD) or, if it were twenty-five years prior to this time, perhaps a few rotls (say, sixty-four cowries).

Does the entire story not remind you of the medicine men we have been looking at in this chapter? It is true that he would be someone from the "shady" side, but whether or not he was a medicine man, he certainly demonstrated the same magical and mysterious qualities. Magic was certainly in his vocabulary, literally and figuratively. The name Dr. Alhaji Bawa is composed of two titles. It is very unlikely that he earned a medical degree, but it is possible that he was a hajji, i.e., a Muslim who had made a pilgrimage to Mecca. He may very well also have considered himself a medicine man, for they were still around in 1974, though they no longer took payments in primitive currency.

Conclusions. The African culture during this primitive money era was rife with the influences of the spirit world, and not just when a person needed a medicine man in order to contact a deceased ancestor or to predict a future event. These superstitions and mystical beliefs were visible in art forms, secret society rituals, animistic beliefs, metallurgical ceremonies, ceremonial dances, marriages and funerals, and fetishes of family, tribe, and village. It was an integral part of life and death.

Kalabar "fash." Looking over the ways in which these superstitions and beliefs were manifested, it is interesting to note that most of them involved the use of primitive money. Even the secret societies, which were common in some areas, had fees associated with them. If, for some reason, we felt that we needed an explanation for these influences, we could merely pass it off by saying, "It be Kalabar 'fash,' and white man no sabi any ting about it."

CHAPTER NINE

Money and Might

"To be clever enough to get a great deal of money, one must be stupid enough to want it." —G. K. CHESTERTON

Power in the hands of kings and tribal chiefs. When one thinks of the various political positions of leadership in the various towns and cities in Western countries, one pictures many levels of intellect, integrity, charisma, compassion, and leadership ability. The circumstances are similar in Africa. During the colonial period in Africa, some kings or tribal chiefs welcomed the European efforts in their country. However, others refused to cooperate at all. Similarly, some chiefs provided a high level of protection and displayed concern for tribal members, while others required a high annual tribute, with little compassion or concern provided in return. In this chapter we shall look at various examples of governance and power that existed within tribes, villages, and kingdoms, and at the connections with money and power.

Symbols of power. Kings and tribal leaders demonstrated and displayed the power that they possessed in numerous ways. *The way they*

and their families dressed was one example of the way they showed power. Dress included their *marks of status*, which they carried everywhere, and their *articles of adornment.* Many did not consider themselves ordinary mortals and their attire reflected that superior status. *Where they lived* was another way power was demonstrated. They usually lived in a palace complex, which was a compound with a number of buildings. A third way in which these men showed their power was by *the size of their army*, if they had one. Few chiefs or kings may have had a standing military or police unit; however, they often were concerned with protecting their tribe, their kingdom, or their possessions. The men that they would place in the field were in many cases slaves or, on occasion, mercenaries. A fourth way in which they displayed power was in *the wealth they possessed and displayed.* They demonstrated this at all times through the size of the entourage and their mode of travel. They might have traveled by donkey, by highly decorated horse, or by foot. The last way in which they displayed their power was *in their courts*, whether a court of law or a royal court befitting a sovereign. They created policies, issued verdicts, and enacted laws that demonstrated the level of power that was in their hands.

Clothes make the man. If "clothes make the man," as proclaimed by Mark Twain, they also make the man's wife and his children when applied to an African royal setting. The clothes might include imported fabrics, but more often were the articles of adornment attached to an appendage. These might be made of brass, copper, iron, tin, wood, ivory, glass, or shells. They might or might not be currency items, but they always signified power.

Copper had a special significance in this context. "In precolonial African societies as a whole, copper was a signifier of status: status in the sense of wealth, prestige, rank, but also . . . the connotation of power."[1] The importance of this is carried further in the notion that more is better. The more jewelry and objects that you carry on your body and the larger those objects are, the more wealth and prestige you display. This includes wives, daughters, and slave women owned by the husband. These items could be worn on the legs, ankles, arms, wrists, waist, and neck. It was not unusual for a Kongo woman to carry twenty-five pounds (11 kg) of copper on her body, much of it being currency. Henry Stanley wrote of the great wealth and status of Chambiri, who loved to boast of his forty wives who carried a total of eight hundred pounds among them.[2] In Burundi, copper wire bangles might cover a woman's leg from ankle to knee. As Eugenia W. Herbert noted, "The literature is replete with references to rulers and their families being laden with copper and brass, some of them so heavily that their arms had to be supported by attendants."[3] In the Congo Basin in what is now Coquilhatville, the Democratic Republic of Congo, Chief M'Kuba was wearing a set of iron *minkata*, or coiled arm or leg rings. He was asked by a visitor if it was awkward to carry out his duties with the iron weights on his legs. He replied that "it suited the dignity of a chief to have a slower and heavier walk than that of ordinary mortals."[4]

Fig. 102 The minkata, made from both iron and brass, is also called a coiled manilla. It was found in the Dem. Rep. of Congo, Nigeria, and Cameroon.

What an impression! In the mid-nineteenth century, William Balfour Baikie was exploring the Kwo'ra River (now called the Niger) and Benue River in Nigeria, and had occasion to meet the oba (a title signifying the king or ruler), several of his wives, and two of his sons—Aje' and Tshu'kuma. Aje' was the memorable one. He visited one day wearing "homemade scarlet-cloth trousers, a scarlet uniform coat, a pink beaver hat, under which, to make it fit, was a red worsted nightcap, no shoes, beads round the neck, and in his hand a Niger-expedition sword."[5] In a similar manner, David Livingstone tells of a tribal leader by the name of Sambanza, who finished a long oration and rose up, "and in going off was obliged by such large bundles of copper rings on his ankles to adopt quite a straddling walk. When I laughed at the absurd appearance he made, the people remarked, 'That is lordship in these parts.'"[6]

Fig. 103 Here is another show of dignity from the Lomami and Lokele with their massive ligandas and other spearheads

More adornment. The warriors in Ethiopia had an interesting mark of status. In 1874 a French artillery officer by the name of Col. Basil Gras designed a new artillery piece. It was called a Gras rifle and used an eleven-millimeter cartridge that was fifty-nine millimeters (2⅜ inches) long. The rifle became very popular, especially in Europe. This rifle and its cartridges were subsequently introduced into what was then called Abyssinia. It was not long before the warriors developed a fascination with the cartridge and began wearing them as ornaments in cartridge belts. They were articles of adornment and also became items of currency. It is interesting to note that these warriors were armed with spears, not rifles, but they recognized the power and prestige of the cartridge.

Fig. 104 The Gras rifle cartridges were used for small purchases in Ethiopia and as items of prestige.

"A man's home is his castle."[7] Before describing the elegant palace of a king, let's take a look at a common Ibo residential setting in southern Nigeria. The head of the compound was the oldest father living there. His quarters were situated at the center, close to the entrance of the compound. It had a circular floor plan composed of one room with mud-brick walls, very small openings for light and circulation of air, a thatched roof, and a low entry door. The door, a special feature of the building, was carved especially for him and indicated his status. Inside was his bed, made of bamboo or packed earth, and a small sitting area. A goatskin rug or a rush mat might have lain on the mud floor. In the rafters were his gourds for water or palm wine, his goatskin bag holding his primitive money, his machete, his knife, and his spear if he owned one. Each of his wives had her own hut with her bed, a sitting area, and a cooking area. Suspended from the rafters in their huts were

cooking utensils, wooden bowls, gourds, and dried vegetables. Each wife took her turn preparing the meals for the husband and brought it to him in his hut. He generally ate alone. The youngest children slept in their mothers' huts. There were separate huts for the other children.[8] The idea of each wife having her own hut was not a simple African tradition, but rather an important African condition. There was often competition between wives. Mungo Park, African explorer and British physician, wrote: "As every man of free condition has a plurality of wives, it is found necessary (to prevent, I suppose, matrimonial dispute) that each of the ladies should be accommodated with a hut to herself; and all of the huts belonging to the same family are surrounded by a fence."[9]

The Ashanti king's palace. The king of the Ashanti was called the Asantehene, and lived in a large palace located in modern-day Ghana. It was imposing, massive, and ornate. It was described as "an immense building of a variety of oblong courts and regular squares [with] entablatures exuberantly adorned with bold fan and trellis work of Egyptian character. They have a suite of rooms over them, with small windows of wooden lattice, of intricate but regular carved work, and some have frames cased with thin gold. The squares have a large apartment on each side, open in front, with two supporting pillars, which break the view and give it all the appearance of the proscenium or front of the stage of the older Italian theaters. They are lofty and regular, and the cornices of a very bold cane-work in alto-relievo. A drop-curtain of curiously plaited cane is suspended in front, and in each we observed chairs and stools embossed with gold, and beds of silk, with scattered regalia."[10] This beautiful edifice was ransacked and burned by the British in 1874 during the Third Anglo-Ashanti War. In 1925 the British built a new palace and presented it as a gift to the king upon his return from exile.

Above: Fig. 105 The former palace of Asantehene was burned and ransacked by the British in 1874. Below: Fig. 106 The British built the exiled king a new palace in 1925; a part became a museum in 1995.

The man about town. The Benin Empire was ruled by a sovereign head of state called the oba. This empire with its oba has existed from the eleventh century. It later became the Kingdom of Benin in the fourteenth century, with its capital at Edo, today's Benin City, Nigeria. (This is in southern Nigeria and should not be confused with the neighboring West African country of Benin.) The Edo area has always been rich in sculptures made of bronze, iron, ivory, wood, and terracotta. Many bronze sculptures were created using the lost-wax casting method we learned about in chapter seven. The oba's palace and grounds were often the site of elaborate ceremonial court life. The grounds also contained other palaces and houses, and the apartments of the courtiers, that is, advisors and officials from the royal court. In 1668 a Dutch writer, Olfert Dapper, described the oba's palace compound as being as large as the land area of the town of Haarlem in the Netherlands.[11]

No small army. The size of their military force helped indicate the level of power enjoyed by kings or tribal chiefs. The Kingdom of Ghana, in the southeastern part of today's Mauritania and the western part of today's Mali, in the mid-eleventh century had their capital in Kumbi. Gold was the basis of the royal economy and the king frequently spent his time and money warring against neighbors that were causing problems or conducting slave raids. He is reported to have been able to place 200,000 men in the field. Of that number, 40,000 were armed with bows and arrows; presumably the remainder only had spears.[12] This fact would certainly prevent smaller kingdoms and other tribes from becoming too aggressive against him. Several centuries later, in the Ashanti Empire located in present-day southern Ghana and southern Côte d'Ivoire (Ivory Coast), gold continued to be the dominant economic force. The army here fielded an extraordinary 204,000 men.[14]

No small army and remarkable wealth. The quantity of wealth that was on display also demonstrated power. The capital city of Kumbi in the Kingdom of Ghana, mentioned above, consisted of two separate cities located within six miles of each other. One was composed of just Muslims and contained a dozen mosques, while the other had what were then referred to as pagans or non-Muslims. The king's palace and the courts were located in the non-Muslim city. From this palace emerges an interesting tale.

In the royal treasury was an immense gold nugget. It was a symbol of majesty and became famous throughout the better part of the civilized world partly because of its massive size and partly because the king tethered his horse to it. It was alleged to have weighed thirty pounds. In the fourteenth century a spendthrift prince is reported to have sold it to traveling merchants from Egypt. "It was said to weigh a ton."[15]

More on wealth. The Ashanti are the largest tribe in Ghana and Côte d'Ivoire, and are a matrilineal society. That means that their tribe is based on the kinship with the mother of the female line. This is one of the few matrilineal tribes in Africa. In 1701–17 their leader was Osei Tutu, who was referred to as the paramount chief. Later this title became king. He unified all of the independent Ashanti chiefdoms along the coast of Ghana and in a part of Côte d'Ivoire. Gold was the currency of the royalty. It was also one of the reasons for the almost perpetual warfare going on since the early 1600s. In the early 1800s they became a big exporter of slaves.

The royalty possessed remarkable wealth. The king was the "heir to the gold of every subject, from the highest to the lowest."[16] His weights when weighing gold were one-third heavier than the weights of others in the country. However, the excess was used to enrich the chamberlain, cook, and the other domestic officers of the palace. The king felt that it was derogatory to pay his subjects for their services. The keeper of the royal treasury took in all of the tributes and revenues on behalf of the king. He was like a chancellor of the exchequer or a secretary of the treasury. He kept all of the records and held the only key to the huge apartment in the palace where all of the gold was stored. This treasurer held court on a daily basis in his own house on all cases affecting revenue or tribute. The king himself was the final appeal and heard very few cases.

This is not a small claims court. When the king heard the cases on appeal, he was generally reclined in his raised bed, with many cushions scattered about, covered with a beautiful rich cloth, and with two or three of his most beautiful wives standing close by. When one public debtor was convicted but was unable to pay the sum of sixteen ounces of gold, the king commuted the sentence to twenty male slaves. There is even a written document that is followed by the Ashanti system of justice and is referred to as a constitution. It contains some interesting "rights." For example, if "a slave seeks refuge from an ally or tributary, he is restored: if from an unconnected power, he is received as a free subject."[17] Another law says that the sisters of the king may "marry or intrigue with whom they please provided he be an eminently strong or personable man."[19] There are no definitions given as to what exactly is meant by "eminently strong" or a "personable man." One more law: if a woman is involved in a "palaver," then she is involving her family but not her husband.[18] A palaver is a discussion between two or more tribespeople that is unnecessarily long and is generally very emotional.

In order to help the king to pay for the royal expenses, the sources of revenue were many and varied:

1. Anyone passing through the kingdom, but who was not a resident, paid a tribute.
2. A tax in gold was levied on all slaves purchased for the coast.
3. Customs were paid in gold by all traders returning from the coast.

4. A tax was levied on elephant hunters.

5. Gold pits in Soko yielded two thousand ounces of gold per month; others yielded seven hundred ounces.

6. Each chief was taxed when he increased the number of gold ornaments he had.

7. The soil in the market place was "washed" twice a year, yielding eight hundred ounces of gold at each washing.

Fig. 107 Gold dust was used in large and small purchases by weight (*mithqal*) or grains, in Ghana, Ivory Coast, and Togo.

Beyond this revenue for the king was the tribute paid annually by each large town and the capitals of the various regions within the kingdom that included five hundred slaves, two hundred cows, four hundred sheep, four hundred cotton cloths and two hundred silk cloths. Smaller towns paid proportionally less.[19] It is clear that all the sources of revenue listed above translated into a tremendous amount of power for the king of the Ashanti.

Guard dogs. The circumstances surrounding the king of the Kingdom of Ghana were not dissimilar to that of the king of the Ashanti. Let's imagine we had an audience with the king at some time in the late nineteenth century. He sat in the center of a massive pavilion, adorned in much jewelry, including a golden headdress. Our arrival would have been accompanied by much ritual and ceremony, with beautiful pageantry. Surrounding the pavilion were ten horses with gold trappings. The throne was large and ten pages stood behind it, holding shields and gold-hilted swords. On the right stood the sons of the vassal princes, magnificently attired, with ornaments plaited into their hair. In front of the king sat high-ranking Muslim officials called viziers. At his feet sat the governor of the city. The king's constant companions, his hound dogs, stood guard over the pavilion wearing collars from which hung small bells of silver and gold. Before any ceremony began, the royal drums, the *deba*, were sounded, and the king's pagan countrymen would kneel before him and commence to pour dust on their heads, while the polite Muslims showed their respect by clapping their hands.[20] We would have received a distinct impression of the wealth, resources, and power of the Kingdom of Ghana.

The royal court of the Mangbetu. Dr. Georg August Schweinfurth, botanist, paleontologist, and an important explorer in east and central Africa, spent several extended periods with the Mangbetu tribe in what is now the Democratic Republic of Congo. He provided a descriptive picture of the royal court of the Mangbetu people. In the nineteenth century this tribe was reputed to be cannibalistic.

Fig. 108 King Munsa is seated at the far end of the royal hall.

Observe the many examples of primitive money: mats, throwing knife, numerous coiled copper items, bangles, numerous spears, necklace, and several unidentified items. There are many dazzling copper pieces that are difficult for us to appreciate in a black-and-white representation. Note the description of the ceremonial arms: "Posts are driven into the ground, and long poles were fastened horizontally across them; then against this extemporized scaffolding were laid, or supported crosswise, hundreds of ornamental lances and spears, all of pure copper, and of every variety of form and shape. The gleam of the red metal caught the rays of the tropical noontide sun, and in the symmetry of their arrangement the rows of dazzling lance-heads shone with the glow of flaming torches, making a background to the royal throne that was really magnificent. This display of wealth, which according to Central African tradition was incalculable, was truly regal, and surpassed anything of the kind that I had conceived possible."[21]

CHAPTER TEN

Money and Mourning

"Keep your lives free from the love of money and be content with what you have." —HEBREWS 13:5

Departing after the pub closes. As the noted Nigerian journalist and author Peter Enahoro says, "When a death occurs in Nigeria, the mourning that follows is usually a game of conventional grief played between the bereaved and sympathizers."[1] The actual practices, though, differed greatly from tribe to tribe within the continent. When the missionaries arrived in the nineteenth century, Western practices were introduced. We saw in chapter five the remarkable work of Mary Slessor. The expenditure on funerals was a tremendous burden on a household already distressed with grief. Most of the village members were expected to participate in the funeral proceedings. Relatives might show up and bring friends along. "Relations who wouldn't give the deceased a drink of water in the middle of the Sahara in his lifetime now turn up with their friends, carrying cartons of beer and demanding attention so everyone can see how much they loved 'Cousin Mustafa.'"[2] A great deal of emphasis was placed on showing respect to the deceased and members of the family. If the deceased was a young man who had died childless, there might be much less fuss over the passing, following the theory that "his spirit was evil." "But if he departs, to use a Churchillian phrase, after the pub closes, then his family are under strict obligation to mark his death in a merry way."[3] Herein lies the expenditure for the family of the deceased. Some of the Ibo of Nigeria show up for the funeral because they want to be sure to receive their "fair share of the heritage."[4] Often tribal chiefs and other important tribe members, both male and female, were buried inside their hut or in its veranda, even though the heirs continued to inhabit the place.[5] A few of the young kinsmen from the mourners volunteered to dig the grave. In the meantime, the body was washed and camwood ointment was applied. The deceased was then dressed in his *riga* and placed on mats on the bottom of the grave. A riga is the long, flowing gown that was considered at that time the traditional dress for men. It is important to note here that whether the deceased was an animist, a Christian, or a Muslim would determine the course followed for the ceremony. The body was generally buried within a twenty-four-hour period. Let's take a look at a traditional animist ceremony for a male, which was likely conducted by the "priest," or medicine man.

In Zora Neale Hurston's *Baracoon*, she cites Kossola, "the last survivor of the last known slave ship: "Bury a man in the ground below his house and he will be at home forever."

An animist ceremony. Some primitive money jewelry, such as a bracelet or necklace, may be worn by a deceased male. Iron bell money may also be included in order to announce his arrival into the spirit world, and food items such as cut-up yams, kola nuts, and cassava could be added. If the deceased was a member of the Mossi tribe in Burkina Faso or the Malinke or Bambara tribes in Mali and Senegal, kola nuts were themselves considered a currency. Sometimes food items sprinkled with the blood of a sacrificial chicken and some broken pots were placed on the top of the grave after it was filled in. In eastern Nigeria, in the region of the Igbo-Ukwu culture, the practice was to bury several slaves along with their master. The slaves were alive; the master was not. If they could afford it, four additional slaves could accompany the master, and a bag of food was entrusted to the female slave. However, in 1854 when the oba of Benin died in the Onitsha area of southeastern Nigeria, it is reported that forty slaves were slaughtered. That is quite a sacrifice, although those slaves were a special purchase; the local authorities did not want to use domestic slaves.[6] Just imagine the total cost and the size of that burial pit!

Fig. 109. A wood carving of the oba, or king, of Benin wearing the traditional beads as a part of the royal costume.

With help to the afterlife, a grave situation. Among the Ashanti in Ghana, when a tribal member of some standing passes away, "gold and other valuable articles [are] deposited with the body in the grave."[7] In some places it is customary for the mourners, as well, to contribute money by depositing it in the grave. Statements such as "This is to help them get to the other side" or "This may get them across the great river" were often made. One may wonder just what prompts some of these traditions. Note here that the situation that we are considering is an animist ceremony. There may be bloodshed, a great deal of fear and anxiety expressed, and evil spirits to be concerned with. The answers to questions that we may have are likely to be found somewhere in the centuries-old African animistic beliefs.

Another grave undertaking. The tradition mentioned above, where "gold and other valuable articles were deposited with the body in the grave," has the tale of a grave robber associated with it. It began with a grave robber and, after a long period of time, and involving kings and chiefs, deception, treachery, intrigue, much bloodshed, it ended with the devastating Ashanti War. Several versions of this account exist. Here's one from the *Mission from Cape Coast Castle to Ashantee* by T. Edward Bowdich.

A traveler named Meredith visited the Ashanti area in 1817, ten years after the following series of events took place. The land area north of the Ashanti Kingdom was called the Assin country, which was divided into two parts. One was ruled by King Cheboo and the other by King Amoo, with each being subordinate to the king of the Ashanti, in present-day Ghana. A very wealthy man died in Amoo's village, and a quantity of gold and valuables was deposited with the body in the grave. A man from Cheboo's village was present and decided to return at a later date and remove those objects of value from the gravesite. He did so and absconded with his treasure. Amoo sought redress with Cheboo, but with no success. He went next to the king of the Ashanti, where an impartial hearing was held, after which the verdict was awarded in favor of Amoo. Now began a series of incidents involving deception, treachery, intrigue, and bloodshed. Amid all of this, the king of the Ashanti tried several times to act as arbitrator to bring peace, once giving a gold manilla to each king and another time a gold sword to each. The gold did not appear to bring about reconciliation, however. If there is a lesson to be learned, it is: be careful where, when, and how you bury money.

How to "bale out." Another tradition associated with burial in parts of Africa is body wrapping, also called a "bale." Body wrapping is one of the methods by which a body could be interred. There are two other methods: (1) placing the body inside a coffin and (2) interring the body with no covering of any kind except for clothing. There was a time when several tribes buried the deceased with no clothing on. The primitive money item called a "cloth" had in some locations three iterations: men's cloths, women's cloths, and burial cloths. The burial cloth was larger, and was either black or white depending on local tradition. The men's or women's cloths were a more common currency, and measured about one-and-a-half by two feet. Inside the hut of the deceased, the body was slowly wrapped in the burial cloths when the mourners delivered them while coming in to pay their respects. The story is told of a male corpse in the Stanley Pool area of the Democratic Republic of Congo that was so lavishly bundled it could not be removed through the doorway. The solution was to simply remove a portion of the exterior mud-brick wall to extricate the "bale" and roll it all the way to the gravesite, where it was planted upright. It was a costly but impressive sight. According to one writer, "A woman never justifies this expense and the maximum number expended on her is about 20 [burial cloths]."[8]

Body painting. Body painting was a common practice in many areas of Africa. The common colors were white, black, red, yellow, and pink. They were produced mostly from local vegetable products. The purpose of body painting was for "medicine" (animist burial ceremonies), social expression, and for purely ornamental reasons. White rings around the eyes were the sign of mourning when a husband, father, or brother passed away. If a young girl was painted white all over, she was in the beginning stages of "fattening" for marriage. When warriors were setting off for a battle, they were painted all black. If a festive occason was coming, the women were very creative. Their makeup might be a simple white mask painted from ear to ear, or might consist of intricate, colorful geometric patterns. When a girl reached the age of puberty and was betrothed to a man, she was painted red all over, signifying that she must cease all intercourse with other men.[9]

Paying the price. Funerals in Africa were costly during the primitive money era. When a "big man" dies there are the expenses for the wife to entertain and possibly house the relatives and friends; in fact, the entire district may show up for the ceremonies. "Thus it often happens that even a 'big woman' is bankrupt by the expense."[10] If there is an inheritance due to the relatives, it is a further financial expense. Beyond this, there are the mats that go on the bottom of the grave, and the mourners' financial obligations. Providing the burial cloths, if that is the local tradition, has been mentioned, as has donating money to get the deceased "over to the other side." These were significant financial matters for the mourner.

How much to give? We shall look now at some of the aspects behind this notion of tossing money into the big hole in the ground. For example, how was the amount determined? The amount that was donated or the form of money donated was dependent on several factors. First is the matter of who passed away. Was he a poor man with a low social standing in the tribe? If so, Kissi pennies, several rotls of cowries, and other low-denomination currency might be deposited. Second, the traditions and norms of the particular tribe would be in play here. It may be simply the common manillas that are the norm. Third, the primitive money that was available and in use in that particular village determined what was offered. Remember that each village had its own stipulations. It may have leaned heavily on iron hoes, as in Nigeria, or on copper items, as in the Democratic Republic of Congo. Finally, the standing of the donor was important. If you were an outstanding member of the community you would be expected to set the pace and give a good example to the others through your donation. Perhaps a Kwadja double hoe, a Bangala spearhead, a beautiful Bwaka throwing knife, a king or queen manilla, or even a few Maria Theresa thalers would be appropriate. In general though, the donation would tend to represent a middle-denomination currency. One of the common manillas may be the expected currency. A Katanga cross is also a likely choice, or several sombe pennies.

Next in line might be one of the many iron pieces like the purr-purr, tajere, idoma or *shoka* if available. In other words, a wide variety of items could have been donated at the gravesite.

Fig. 110 Bwaka throwing knife, made of forged iron, was one of the most aesthetically pleasing designs.

Fig. 111 The king (above left) and queen (right) manillas were more of a store of value than a general trade currency. They were important also in paying bride-price.

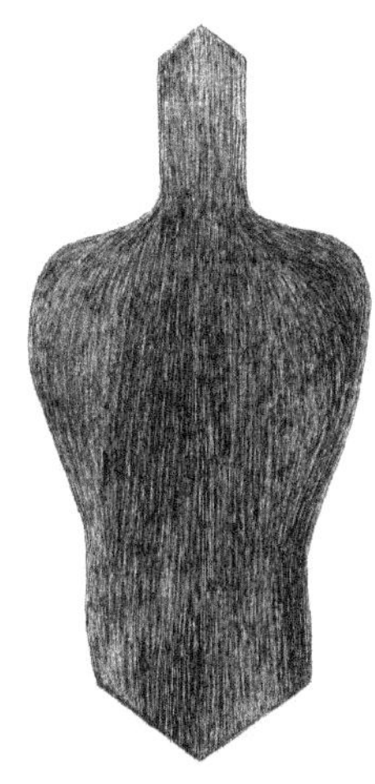

Fig. 112 Shoka. The name means "axe" or "hoe." The first implements came from Birmingham, England, and were originally made from inferior-grade sheet iron. The Mangbetu blacksmiths then made their own.

The Fangs plan ahead, but not much mourning. The Fang are a large tribe located in the rainforest regions of Cameroon, Equatorial Guinea, Gabon, Republic of Congo, and São Tomé and Príncipe. Historically, they practiced cannibalism. Mary H. Kingsley, a British nurse, traveled through the area, and recorded that she limited the number of Fangs in her entourage to just three because they had to go through long stretches of uninhabited forest. Her concern was losing control of the group. The Fang had the reputation that they would kill people, including the traders who ventured through their region, and "cut them up into neat pieces, eat what they want at the time, and smoke the rest of the bodies for future use."[11] Kingsley did not want to be a part of those neat pieces.

Fig. 113 Mary H. Kingsley was an English nurse, explorer, writer, and ethnologist. She traveled throughout West Africa and died in South Africa at thirty-seven.

They traveled to one of the Fang villages, where she was given a hut to sleep in by the chief. Before falling asleep, she noticed a violent odor that was of an organic origin. After an investigation, she found that it was located in one of the porter's bags. Not wanting to lose any valuable items, she shook the contents out, using her hat as a receptacle. Out came a human hand, three big toes, four eyes, two ears, and an assortment of other body parts. The human hand was fresh; the other parts were a bit shriveled. One of her porters expressed what he thought was a common-sense attitude toward his eating habits. First of all he claimed that man's flesh was very good to eat, and he wished the white person would try it. And no, he does not eat his relations; he really does not do this! However, he will eat his next-door neighbor's relations and will in turn sell his own deceased relatives to his next-door neighbor. He further wants us to know that he does not buy slaves and fatten them up for his table. Mary H. Kingsley must have felt a bit uneasy when it was time for "chop" with her little expedition, seeing she would be the one in charge and responsible for providing the food.

CHAPTER ELEVEN
Money and Monetization

"In 2008 the U.S. Bureau of Engraving and Printing used about 18 tons of ink per day between the D.C. and Fort Worth facilities."

—BUREAU OF ENGRAVING & PRINTING

Primitive money did have limitations. At this point we have two goals. The first is to make a general evaluation of primitive money in Africa beyond the one given in chapter one relating to the functions and characteristics of money. The second is to give the numerous steps that took place in one African region during the transition from primitive money to a system of coinage, a process that may be referred to as monetization. Before we look into those issues, however, let us set some parameters. At some of the larger ports of entry, especially in West African ports, the prices of goods were often greatly influenced by the large trading companies, which also manipulated the values of the commodities. They did this by delaying or accelerating the purchases of certain exports and by being cautious about what goods were made available through importation. Therefore, they controlled the currency. A separate issue was that some of the larger coastal towns were accustomed to the use of world coinage, such as the Maria Theresa thalers and a few other coins, which were used and welcomed by most coastal people. Therefore, the examination of any limitation of primitive money will exclude the coastal areas because of these factors. With this in mind, we will look at some of the issues or problems that stood out with respect to primitive money.

The inconvenience of cowries. In the early 1920s in the Bauchi area of central Nigeria, federal taxes were paid in cowries. The rate at the time was four thousand cowries to the shilling, with five shillings' worth being roughly a donkey load. At that time, one British pound was twenty shillings, and each shilling was twelve pence. In Bauchi, there was a store of cowries that was getting so large as to be nearly unmanageable. Therefore, the pressure was on the local authorities to move them out, to somehow get rid of them. The irony of all of this was that cowries were no longer considered legal tender in that region. However, we must not ignore the power of the devoted market folk who would not give up on them. Legal tender or not, the reality was that thousands and thousands of cowries had to be counted, and their total value wasn't much more than a few British pounds. "It was a ridiculous spectacle to see the entire native staff assiduously counting a shilling!"[1]

The element of "willing parties" is necessary in a transaction. There are countries in the Western Hemisphere where you may buy a large appliance such as a refrigerator, and demand that you be allowed to pay for this in the lowest-denomination legal tender. It may mean that you bring a wheelbarrow full of copper coins to complete your payment. The law allows for this kind of transaction. The denomination of your payment can be determined by either buyer or seller. There must be agreement, however. The same idea holds true in Africa. The trader in the market may simply refuse to sell to you unless you pay for her goods using her preferred commodity. Certainly there was often frustration with a system where you had money with which to purchase goods, but your money was refused. The reality of the situation, however, is that when you went to the market, you generally were aware of what was expected for payment. It is those other times, when you are not aware of the expected currency, that can bring on the frustration. One example of this unexpected demand is the Englishman who crossed over to the western shore of Lake Tanganyika in 1874 and was surprised to learn that his trade beads were not honored in any purchases. He used his Katanga crosses instead, but going west he found that, in the next village, those were not honored either. There was no uniformity from one village to the next. Each village had, in effect, its own system of currency. This was true on the entire continent. For the Englishman on Lake Tanganyika there was no Salvation Army and no British Consulate available from which to seek help. He had plenty of money, just the wrong kind, so he was "utterly strand-ed."[2]

The demise of the primitive money era in Africa was no small matter. There were prognosticators from the West in the nineteenth century who said that, given a choice, the people in Africa would be anxious to see a change in their system of currency. It must be admitted that there were many places in Africa that did welcome the official introduction of a national or regional coinage system. These were usually coastal areas, and were already using a world coinage system during the demise of the old system. In some cases, these areas were using the new modern coinage simultaneously with the old system. The world coinage was composed of Maria Theresa thalers, Spanish doubloons, or U.S. eagles. However, most references note that people had significant difficulty in converting from the primitive system to a modern coinage system. The European traders such as the Royal Niger Company (1886–1900) were anxious to see a demise of the old localized primitive system because of the lack of stability with the rate of exchange within the village itself and also the lack of uniformity and the lack of stability from village to village.[4] To them, it was a hindrance to trade.

A. Hingston Quiggin tells a story from this time of transition in Nigeria. In 1900 the British introduced some English silver coins into Nigeria, and they were so successful that they immediately withdrew them. The coins had been so eagerly accepted because the women made them into personal jewelry, and "headdresses of shillings became the latest fashion."[3] This is a good time to remind the reader that even though we are addressing the demise of primitive money here, the barter system in Africa never did truly disappear. It was especially alive and well among the European traders and the local people in West Africa.

Help or hindrance. The lifespan of primitive money in Africa was approximately five hundred years, from the fifteenth to the twentieth century. There is not an abundance of information available on the subject of primitive money. It has been stated that "the natural history of money is an almost virgin subject."[5]

We'll now look at whether primitive money helped or hindered the progress of civilization during that period. Did the use of these commodities encourage development and evolution within the communities where they were used or were they impediments to progress? We are concerned now with economic development, social progress, and general historical trends that may have been associated with the use of primitive money. We'll take a look at the sociological, technical, artistic, and agricultural implications.

Positive influence. Primitive money was a "vehicle" by which progress can be seen in many aspects of African society. What the metallurgists have done with iron and copper is astounding and they have been doing it for centuries. Artistically, there is a reason why collectors and galleries are so attracted to examples such as the Mbole hollow leg band and the various throwing knives and spearheads. All are marvelous examples of the exquisite artistic talent on display throughout Africa, as well as highly developed smithing techniques. Consider also the exquisite individual designs of the thousands of pieces of Kuba or raffia cloth mats. They are pleasing to the eye and have become collectors' items in their own right. Primitive money in the form of tools and weapons sometimes still had a function. A few were still used in farming, hunting, and warfare. The throwing knives, for example, had a physical function as well as an artistic one, and that function helped in determining design.

A "rainy day" notion. Was village life in any way improved by primitive money? Comparing the eighteenth century to the twentieth century, the earlier period was a distinctly subsistence mode. Food was grown to feed the family. At some point in the evolution of their system, people began to see the possibility of putting money aside for later use: a "rainy day" fund. This gave an added purpose for the acquisition of money.

Enter the female marketplace trader. A new sense of purpose developed for these vendors with a goal of "saving" money. There was a passion for work that kept the women at the market from early morning until dusk. Some may argue whether this is progress or not. If it represents the early stages of capitalism, it may be a good question for the reader to contemplate.

The negative influence of primitive money. One negative aspect is perhaps the tradition of the female members of a household displaying the wealth of the senior male member. When currency items of copper or brass of great total weight were hammered onto the neck, arms, or legs of women, they were "permanent evidences of deluded vanity."[6]

Fig. 114 Konga leg band on legs. The Konga leg band is not easily removed; note support needed at feet.

Fig. 115 Igbo brass anklet disk. The massive brass anklet disc was heavy and awkward; the tube housing the ankle extended 1½ inches (4 cm) above and also below the disc.

Another negative aspect is the "cattle cult" of Kenya and Tanzania. Those wealthy cattle owners were not always concerned with the health of their animals or the erosion of their soil due to overgrazing practices, but rather with how many heads of cattle they owned.

The passing of a time-honored currency system in British West Africa. British West Africa was composed of present-day Nigeria, Ghana, Sierra Leone, and the Gambia. The primitive money that had stood so firmly for many centuries was showing signs of weakness. Remember two facts concerning this legal tender: (1) it was sanctioned by the rulers, be they Islamic or civil, and (2) the people had accepted it, inconveniences and all. There was a sense of ownership, in other words. A transition to a monetary system using coins from a highly entrenched system such as the one that existed in West Africa was not to be accomplished with a single action or a set of short-sighted actions. It needed patient, long-term planning and execution.

To better understand the collapse of the primitive monetary system, let's look at a time line leading up to its demise, concentrating mostly on British West Africa:

1. In 1807 the slave trade was banned in the United Kingdom, giving less importance to cowries and manillas as currencies.

2. In 1863 Abraham Lincoln emancipated the slaves, and in 1865 the

Thirteenth Amendment made it illegal to own slaves in the United States of America.

3. In the mid-1880s several European countries shipped 35,000 tons of cowries to West Africa. Prices crashed, and in some locations it spelled the end of cowries as currency.

4. In 1902 the Native Currency Proclamation prohibited the importation of manillas. It was intended to promote world coinage like thalers, doubloons, and eagles.

5. In 1912 the West African Currency Board introduced coinage to be used alongside primitive money.

6. In 1919 the Manilla Currency Ordinance was passed, prohibiting foreign traders from using manillas in any transactions.

7. In 1948 manillas were abolished and then redeemed for scrap. They redeemed 32.5 tons for 436 British pounds sterling. It was not considered successful.

8. On April 1, 1949 the manilla was no longer legal tender in West Africa.

Notice in this time line that there are only three denominations of primitive currency involved in the process: slaves, cowrie shells, and manillas. The imported cowrie shells and manillas were used in the purchase of slaves for export, so slaves were one of the keys. The British must be commended for their leadership in banning slavery and in turning back slave ships to port and thereby helping to turn the world attitude toward slavery around.

Despite item three above, cowries were in a class by themselves. In 1900 (twenty years after the 35,000 tons of cowries were shipped in) the Nigerian government was still giving exhortations and prohibitions regarding cowrie shells. They finally took a stand and allowed no more importation of cowrie shells. This had two distinct effects: the resolve of the people to continue using the cowries increased greatly, and the value of the cowrie shells soared. This is the opposite of what the government was trying to achieve. The traders in the markets would either give a better value when cowries were offered, or in some cases simply refused to deal with anything except cowries.[7]

A short history of the WACB. The West African Currency Board was formed in 1912, with headquarters in London. They did several things that certainly helped in the transition to coinage. First, they allowed coins and paper currency to be used at the same time as the primitive money was in use. This was a good psychological approach, and it allowed for a unified system of coinage to be put into place through their action. Their official responsibility was for production and distribution of currency in the four British West African colonies of the Gambia, Sierra Leone, Ghana, and Nigeria. Second, they established various central banks, including the Central Bank of Nigeria (CBN) in 1959. This bank created a monetary authority that was charged with setting up the institutional machinery necessary to lead the region into the monetization of the economy. The first actions of the WACB in 1912 were to encourage use of the British silver shilling and copper penny, and they minted the WACB one-tenth penny in London.

Above: Fig. 116 The copper 1907 one-tenth penny minted in London for the WACB.

Right: Fig. 117 The use of the 1912 British copper penny was encouraged by the WACB.

175

Above: Fig. 118 The four countries of the WACB were encouraged to use the British silver one-shilling coin (1902).

Above: Fig. 119 One of the first paper issues of the WACB was the two-shilling note (1918). Below: Fig. 120 Another of the first issues from the WACB was the ten-shilling note (1916).

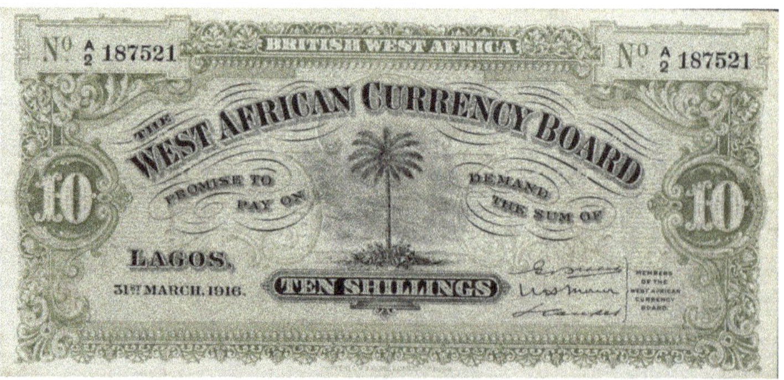

The first paper issues from the WACB were in 1916: the two-, ten-, and twenty-shilling notes. However, in 1918 there was a little confusion. The board was unable to keep up with the demand for the one-shilling notes, so they printed 21 million additional ones in London. After waiting for several months for the London shipment to arrive, the demand was so great that the Nigerian authorities printed their own in Lagos. When the salmon-colored notes finally arrived from London, the local ones were withdrawn.

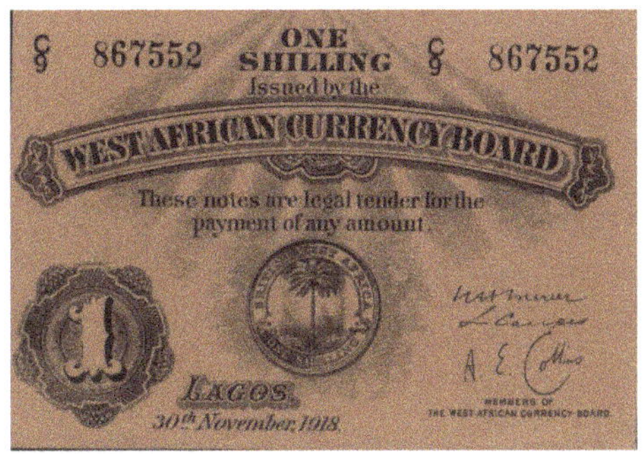

Above: Fig. 121 There was a shortage of the salmon-colored one-shilling notes in Nigeria, so 21 million additional were printed (1918).
Below: Fig. 122 The demand for one-shilling notes was so great and Nigeria couldn't wait, so they temporarily printed their own (1918).

In 1919 London began to wonder if West Africa was ready for paper money. Forgeries were becoming more prevalent. The 1928 series was issued from 1928 to 1951. The ten- and twenty-shilling notes were printed on paper that was of greatly improved quality and incorporated watermarks.

Above: Fig. 123 Forgeries inspired the WACB to issue the 1928 series of new ten-shilling notes (1941).

Above: Fig. 124 The newly inspired twenty-shilling notes had watermarks and improved paper quality (1934)

The early 1950s was the time of discovery. Sierra Leone discovered large iron ore deposits and diamonds; Ghana discovered gold, manganese, and diamonds; and Nigeria discovered oil. This all inspired the redesign of the ten- and twenty-shilling notes. Scenes from nature were a part of this. Shortly after they were first issued, they added a security thread to help with the counterfeiting problem.

Above: Fig. 125 The early 50s series ten-shilling note was redesigned with a security thread added (1953).

Above: Fig. 126 Beautiful scenes from nature were shown on the 50s series notes, including the twenty-shilling note (1957).

Fig. 127 The large-size hundred-shilling/five-pound note was reintroduced by the WACB (1954).

The CBN's research department wrote a several-hundred-page report that referred to the initial efforts made in 1912 as signifying a breakthrough in the overall effort to see a transition into a coinage system in West Africa. In 1962, fifty years after the formation of the West African Currency Board and three years after the formation of the Central Bank of Nigeria, there were still tons of manillas in circulation in Nigeria. It is difficult to call this a breakthrough. This same report concluded: "The process of monetization . . . has been a protracted one."[8] Indeed, it was prolonged and drawn-out in traditional government fashion.

PART II

Details

Data, Image, and Citation Index

Names & Details	Image	Citations	Tribe/Country
BANGALA SPEARHEAD. Not a weapon, only as money. Few details are available.		Quiggin 65, Ballarini 120,121, Opitz 313, 314, Mitton 102, Robertson 6.	Lobelle, Ngbaka-Bwaka, Democratic Republic of Congo (DRC).
BEADS, AGGRY. There is disagreement among the authorities. The true aggry was a blue tubular bead.		Leonard 56, Opitz 38, 39, Quiggin frontispiece, 36–40, Wieschhoff 31, 34, Mitton 101.	Many tribes in West Africa, including Nigeria, Benin, Ghana. At times confused with millefiori or chevron beads.
BEADS, HEBRON. (KANO). Earth tones of yellow, green, and blue. Made in Hebron using Dead Sea salts.		Mitton 108, Opitz 51, Scott Semans list.	Found in the Sudan and in Kano, Nigeria. The Sudanese called them mongur beads.
BEADS, MILLEFIORI. A glass bead of varying lengths, colors, shapes, and patterns.		Leonard 56, 57, Mitton 113, Opitz 38, Quiggin 39 (described but not named), Aumann 32, 33.	One of the best-known trade beads throughout much of Africa; made in Venice in the late 1800s.
BEADS, MUNSHI. Tiny seed-shaped brass beads that are on average 12 mm long. Very cute.		Quiggin 59, 60, Opitz 41, Mitton 104, Reed 8, Johansson 50, 54 and supplement 14 #65.	Munshi is another name for the Tiv of central Nigeria.

Names & Details	Image	Citations	Tribe/Country
BEADS, OSTRICH EGGSHELL (BUSHMAN'S BEADS). Tough shells 5–8 mm in diameter. One of the oldest bead types.		Leonard 49, Mitton 117, Opitz 59, 60, 246, Quiggin 100, 107, Wieschhoff 13.	Maasai of East Africa, Turkana of Kenya, Ovambo & Samburu in Namibia & Angola, the Bushmen of Namibia, Angola.
BOLKO (OKANU, KONGA). Dimensions vary: 40.6 cm high (16"), 26 cm wide (10 ¼"). Weight: 1.22 kg (2 lbs. 11 oz).		Quiggin 68, Opitz 88, 89, Leonard 83, Joyce 25, Fig. 40.	The blacksmiths from Nkutshu tribe made these for the Songo Meno tribe, DRC.
BUBU THROWING KNIFE. Has about 12" length with a large 6" disc at end of stem. Not a weapon, only money.		Quiggin 70, Opitz 350, Kierans 6, 7.	Bubu tribe on the northern shores of the Ubangi River in the DRC.
BWAKA THROWING KNIFE. 41.3 cm x 29.2 cm x 1.3 cm (16.25" x 11.5" x 0.5"). Made of iron with a copper wrap.		Leonard 87, Opitz 181, 183, Quiggin 69, Mitton 104, Joyce 19, Figure 25.	Bwaka, Ngbaka of DRC, Mabo, Nzombo of DRC, and Central African Republic.
CALABAR RODS (OKPOHO OKUK). A brass rod 1 yard long bent into a U shape. Weighs 1 ½ lbs.		Eyo 64, 67, Fry 174, Herbert (Red Gold) 134–138, 195, Hutchinson 255, Opitz 99, 244, 287, Partridge 253, Posnansky 5, Reed 30, Quiggin 87.	Used by the Efik tribe in Old Calabar, Nigeria, from about 1698 to 1907.

Names & Details	Image	Citations	Tribe/Country
CALICO (DOTIS). Different dimensions in different tribes. Often 10–12 in. x 2 yards (25.4–30.5 cm x 183 cm).		Barth 323, Dugard 125, Einzig (1966) 128, Quiggin 59.	Zimbabwe: bride price, wages, & burial. Stanley used this currency on the way to Ujiji, Tanzania.
CARTRIDGE. They were of the popular Gras rifle. Cartridges as currency were used from the 1800s to 1930s.		Einzig (1966) 115; Sigler 18; Reed 88; Mitton 104; Opitz 102.	Warriors in Ethiopia used cartridges as ornaments in cartridge belts and as currency. They were armed with spears but not rifles
CATTLE. Often the term used for sheep, goats, cows, or camels. References break down large stock from small.		Einzig (1966) 110, 117, 122; Eyo 55; Guyer 250; Leonard 15; Melitz 98; Mitton 104; Opitz 104; Quiggin 33, 92, 93; Sigler 13, Kierans 10.	Dinka, Shilluk, and Nuer in the Sudan, the Maasai in Kenya.
CHEETEM, SITIM, USITIM. Strands of copper or brass wire 45.7 cm (18") long and bent in half.		Johansson 43, 44, Einzig (1966) 118, 121, Dugard 125, Fry 174, Hutchinson 123, Kingsley 45, Leonard 82, 83 Ngam 22, Opitz 308, Quiggin 88.	Efiks of Old Calabar; Stanley carried this wire with him in search of Dr. Livingstone.
CLOTHS: MALE, FEMALE, BURIAL. (GABAGA, LANGTANG, KUNTU, PAWN). Strips in blanket are 21 cm x 224 cm (8 ½" x 88").		Quiggin 33, 34, 46, 55, 63, 85, Ryder 40, Eyo 56, Opitz 107, Quiggin 88, Eyo 67, 108, Melitz 98, Johannson 51 Einzig (1949) 153, Einzig (1966) 111, 121, Battuta 338, Wieschoff 34, Mitton 104, Kierans 8.	Much of Africa had cotton cloths of some form, including cloths for wrapping a corpse.

Names & Details	Image	Citations	Tribe/Country
CONGO LEG BAND (RIDGED CRESCENT). 13 cm x 4 cm (5¼" x 1¾"), 1.62 kg (3 lb 4 oz), cast & forged brass with 3 ridges.		Opitz 124, 202 and 277, 278, Scott Semans listing.	Ngata, Kutu, and Kela, Dem. Rep. of Congo.
COWRIE SHELLS. 1.5–2.5 cm (5/8"–1") shallow water mollusk *Cypraea moneta* & *Cypraea annulus* from Maldive Islands.		Einzig (1949) 147, Eyo 58, Baikie 416, Langa 33, Einzig (1966) 124, Fry 174, Hutchinson 254, Kriger 170, Melitz 98, Sigler 12, Nitsche 17, 19, Glaze 166–169, Guyer 39, Opitz 118–121, Quiggin 29–34, Shaw 261, 262, Stearns 300, Leonard 65, Mitton 105, Bleeker 59, Wieschhoff 8.	Found in many tribes and countries.
DOUBLE GONG (ILONGA, GUNGA ELOUNDIA). Sizes & dimensions vary. This is about 27 cm (10 ¾") wt. 395 g (14 oz).		Ballerini 113, Quiggin 74, 75, Melitz 108, Opitz 81, Aumann 48, Robertson 4.	Many tribes and countries from Togo to East Africa, including the DRC.
DUBIL. Length about 38 cm (15"), wt. about 369 g (13 oz), has the shape of a pry bar.		Opitz 135, 136, Joyce 22, Fig. 33, 34, Ryder 98, Eyo 54, Robertson 5.	Sukur tribe of Dubil, Duval, Li (Madagali area) in NE Nigeria.
ENSUBA. It is over 30 cm (1') in length and has wt. of about 6.8 kg (15 lbs.). There was also a triangular ensuba in the Cameroon highlands.		Sigler 16, Leonard 90, Mitton 107, Opitz 140, 141.	Bizom, in east Cameroon. A similar artifact was in Gabon and Angola.

Names & Details	Image	Citations	Tribe/Country
FAN AXES AND FANG AXES. Only about 13 cm (5") in length including the imitation axe-head; in bundles of 10 called ntet or bikei.		Kingsley 59, 320, Mitton 107, Opitz 141, 142, Reed 21, Quiggin 70–72, Eyo 33.	Fan, Fang, and Mpongwe tribes of Gabon, the Pangwe and Pahuin tribes of DRC.
GIN CURRENCY (JINI, IGBA). Tribal chiefs were known to store gin by the case. It appreciated in value.		Einzig (1949) 149, Partridge 253, Mitton 107, Sigler 13, 14, Johansson 47, 48, Guyer 138, Opitz 149, Kierans 8, Fry 5, Eyo 58.	In the Calabar region of Nigeria and also in the DRC.
GOLD DUST. Used for large & small purchases, either by weight (mithqal) or by counting the grains		Leonard 11, 12, Reed 98, Quiggin 29, Opitz 150, Mitton 108, Guyer 35, 98, 99, Bowdich 330, Kierans 9, Sigler 16, 17.	Ashanti of Ghana, Baule and Mande of Côte d'Ivoire, Akan of Ghana and Côte d'Ivoire. Togo was also represented.
IDOMA. Flat, tapered cast iron piece with textured surface flared to a 24 cm (9 ½") triangle; 67 cm (27") long.		Joyce 23, Fig. 37, Scott Semans list, Robertson 6.	Hausa of Yola State, Nigeria, the Idoma of Dutsi District, Kaduna State, Nigeria, also in Liberia.
IKONGA SPEAR-HEAD Iron blade & haft is 63 cm (25"). Total length 178 cm (70"), incl. shaft. Weight is 640 g (1 lb. 6.5 oz).		Aumann 45, Melitz 108, Opitz 161, 163, Quiggin 65, Kriger 89.	The Upper Loma-mi and the Upper Sankuru Rivers in DRC.

Names & Details	Image	Citations	Tribe/Country
KATANGA CROSS (HANDA CROSS, BALUBA CROSS, ST. ANDREWS CROSS). Copper, 16.6 cm x 19 cm (6½" x 7½") weight 818 g. (1 lb. 13 oz.).		Ballarini 119, Aumann 49, Herbert (Red Gold) 186, Opitz 124, Nitsche 25, Eyo 36, Wieschhoff 16, Sigler 17, Quiggin 77–79, Leonard 82, Kierans 10, Mitton 110, 111, Robertson 10, Reed 7.	Kasai and Lomami on southern edge of DRC. Quiggin: "Found from the Cape to Cairo, from Mombasa to Boma."
KING & QUEEN MANILLAS. King: bottom, 26 cm x 16.5 cm (10¼" x 6½"); queen: top, 18.4 cm x 10.2 cm (7¼" x 4").		Johansson 19, Opitz 214, Leonard 77, Quiggin 90, 91, Pl. 1 #14, Eyo 49, 61, Kierans 9.	The king & queen manillas were more of a store of value than a currency of use. So, specific tribes may not have adopted them.
KISSI PENNIES (KILINDI). Flat iron bars with ends flanged, 30–44 cm (11¾–17 ½") in length.		Eyo 33, 34, Opitz 179, 180, Quiggin 92, Aumann 47, Sigler 14, Reed 97, Wieschhoff 15, Mitton 111, Robertson 11, Kierans 9.	Kissi tribe is on the Atlantic between Sierra Leone and Liberia; Toma tribe is in Guinea, also on Atlantic Coast.
KOLA NUTS (GORO, GORA). The nut is about 5 cm (2") in length. Is high in caffeine. Has a ceremonial & a social function.		Einzig (1966) 136, Aumann 29, Opitz 188, Mitton 111, Kierans 8, Wieschhoff 39 (not regarded as money).	Mossi in Burkina Faso, the Malinke and Bambara both of Mali and Senegal.
KONGA LEG-BAND (JAMPIERE). Height: 9¼", diameter 5¼", weight 3.74 kg (8 lb 4 oz).		Opitz 201, 202, Ngam 18, Ballarini 116, Semans list, Mitton 111.	Mongo in the Republic of Congo, the Ekonda in the DRC, and the Igbo of Nigeria.

Names & Details	Image	Citations	Tribe/Country
KUBA CLOTH, (MAT MONEY, MADIBA RAFFIA CLOTH). Made from leaves of the raffia palm. Mat is 45 cm x 39 cm (18" x 16").		Guyer 39, 47, Kriger 170, Melitz 98, Opitz 109–111, Quiggin 57, 79, Reed 27, 68, Mitton 113, Robertson 7.	Kuba Kingdom, DRC, and Lele tribe; also in DRC.
KWADJA DOUBLE HOE (MAMBILA, SUU, AND SO). Cast iron, 66 cm (26") length and weighs a hefty 2 kg (4 lb 8 oz).		Ballarini (1998) 3, Joyce 23, Fig. 35, Opitz 157, 158, Ngam 5, Kriger 99, Robertson 6.	The border region between Mbbem and Yamba, Cameroon, and Mfumte, Nigeria.
LIGANDA (NGBELE, NDOA) Spear made of sheet iron, 1.47–1.68 m long (4'10"–5'6"). They weigh up to 2 kg (4½ lb).		Opitz 203, Eyo 35, Leonard 88, Aumann 43, Quiggin 64, Ballarini 40, 41, Wieschhoff 17, Robertson 10.	Made by the Turumba or the Burumbu for the Lomami, Lokele, or the Manyema, all in DRC.
LUBA ZAPOZAP (KASUYU). Iron axe with wood handle and copper wrap, 40 cm (16") length, axe-head protrudes 15 cm (6").		Eyo 32, Quiggin 63, 64, Opitz 18–20, Melitz 98, Joyce 17, Fig.16, 17, Mitton 125.	Lulua tribe and the Luba tribe in the Songe region of DRC.
MANDJANG (ZONG, BITCHIE). Made of sheet iron, 50 cm h. x 42 cm w. x 2.54 cm d. (19½" x 16½" x 1"). Weight is very light. Only used as currency.		Joyce 23, Fig. 36, Opitz 209, Guyer 78–93, Mitton 113.	Kwele of the Republic of Congo and the Kwele-Bakwele of Gabon.

Names & Details	Image	Citations	Tribe/Country
MANGBETU THROWING KNIFE. This knife is likely one of the trombash family. 36.8 cm x 20.3 cm x 7.6 cm (14½" x 8" x 3").		Quiggin 68, Opitz 357, Joyce 16, Fig. 13, Semans list.	Mangbetu of the DRC.
MANILLAS. Shown are 8 of the 9 common manillas made of copper or copper alloy, 5.5 cm x 9.5 cm (2¼" x 3¾").		Johannson 11–15, Opitz 209–213, Sigler 14, Quiggin 6, 78, 89, Leonard 74–77, Herbert (1984) 201–204, Eyo 61–62, Einzig 150, Baikie 356, Hutchinson 255, Posnansky 1, Ryder 40.	Manillas and cowrie shells are the most accepted tribal currency in all of Africa. Found in many tribes and countries.
MARRIAGE HOE. This was made solely for bride price. Opitz says it is of copper and Leonard says iron.		Mitton 108, Opitz 158, 159, Leonard 25, Quiggin 98.	The Madi tribe from the border area of southern Sudan and Uganda. This was a high-end item that was valued at 10 shillings.
MBOLE HOLLOW LEGBAND (EHUKE, DIAKO). Five different sizes in copper. 19 cm dia. (7.5"), 9 cm depth.		Ballarini 116, Joyce 24, Fig. 38, Opitz 201, Semans list, Mitton 112.	Several tribes: Mbole, Jonga, Mongo, Nkutshu, and Njonge. All located along the Congo River in DRC.
MINKATA (NJA, COILED MANILLA, IDANG). Heavy arm or leg coils of iron or brass as body decoration and currency.		Eyo 64, 65, Mitton 114, Opitz 223, Quiggin 80, Semans list, Joyce 25, Fig. 39.	Wangata tribe on Congo R., Mbandaka, DRC, also the Ugbahn in Igboland, Nigeria, and also found in Cameroon.

Names & Details	Image	Citations	Tribe/Country
MITAKO (TEKE). 8 cm (3") heavy copper or brass rings joined together. It was often different lengths at different times & places.		Quiggin 34, 47, 64, 66, 67, 76, Pl. 2 #1, Wieschhoff 16, Opitz 224, Guyer 7, 40, 49, Reed 108, Ballarini 119, Mitton 114.	Bangala tribe in the Kasai River area of Congo Basin.
MOCK SHIRTS, LARGE AND SMALL (BATAKARI). The shirts were white cotton, coarse weave, & sleeveless.		Einzig (1949) 152, Eyo 69, Johannson 51, Johannson Supplement 14, Quiggin 56, 59.	Bura and Pabir tribes in Bornu Province Nigeria.
MUNSEIA. There is a set of 4 iron blades: 1st nkwa value ½ 2nd bokona value 1 3rd lingeme value 2 4th munseia value 4		Opitz 231, Mitton 114.	Information is lacking on this currency made up of iron blades, but it was used in the DRC.
MUNSHI AXE-HEAD. The object is about 12" in length. Not known if it is iron, copper, or bronze.		Quiggin 88, 89, Pl 1 #8, Opitz 231, Mitton 114, Semans list, Johansson 50, Johansson Supplement 16, Eyo 50.	The Tiv are in east/central Nigeria. The Munshi is another name for the Tiv.
NARROW HOE. Cast iron, 39 cm x 3.7 cm (15½" x 3½"), with weight of 538 g. (1 lb. 3 oz.). Has tang for a wooden handle.		Ballarini (1998) 20, Opitz 159, Semans list.	Several tribes in central and northern Nigeria, Kwele of Gabon.

Names & Details	Image	Citations	Tribe/Country
NEEDLE MONEY (HAKUNA/ ANYUN). Tiny iron currency of about 12 mm length and twice the value of cowrie shells.		Kierans 9, Aumann 46, Quiggin 88, Opitz 238, Eyo 54, Johansson 42, 45, Supp.13, Ngam 17, Mitton 115.	The Ibo tribe used them in Enugu, Nigeria, calling them anyun. Also used in Ethiopia.
NGOMBE THROWING KNIFE, (NGWOLO). Forged iron blade. There is no written history of the Ngombe tribe, so little description.		Opitz 349, 350, Ballarini 76, 77, Aumann 45.	Ngombe, Lingombe, Bagondo, DRC.
NUPE BRACELET, LG. & MED. White brass with 8-facet body and 13-facet ends. LG: 9 cm (3½"), wt. 532 g (18.8 oz); MED: 6.6 cm (2 5/8"), wt. 130 g.		Semans list, Opitz 278, 280, Mitton 116.	Nupe, in Bida, Niger State, Nigeria. Both items have been worn but are attractive.
OGOJA PENNIES (EFUFY, IYAYAW, YAKARO). This iron, Y-shaped currency was 18 cm–28 cm (8¼"–11") tall.		Eyo 33, 51, Leonard 90, Opitz 243, 244, Johansson 36, Supp. 12, Reed 30, Ngam 23, Kierans 9, Mitton 116, Quiggin 87.	Tiv tribe in Benue and Plateau states of Nigeria; the Akuju and Nkumm tribes from other states of Nigeria.
ONGANDA. A bullion item of darkly toned brass with four flat facets, 27–32cm (10½"–12½") long & 1.25–2.5 kg.		Opitz 245, Mitton 116, Semans list, Ballarini 114.	From the Jonga and Mongo tribes of the DRC.

Names & Details	Image	Citations	Tribe/Country
PROTO-MANILLA. This brass or copper form could be the original form of the manilla.		Posnansky 5, Ngam 21, Johansson 14, Fig. 2, Supp. 8 and Figures 32, 33, Opitz 209.	Thought to be a prototype of later manillas. It was excavated at Igbo Ukwu near Onitsha, Nigeria, in 1964 by Prof. Shaw.
PURR-PURR. A flat cast-iron length with a textured surface bent at a 45° angle. Total length 23 cm (9").		Johansson 41, Fig. 12, Supp. 13, #53, Mitton 117, Opitz 273, Semans list, Eyo 54.	The Gwosa from Nigeria. Johansson refers to the tribe as the "hill pagans."
ROUND HOE (KWASUNTING). A cast-iron bowl-shaped hoe with a 15 cm (6") diameter and a tang to hold a handle.		Opitz 158, Mitton 111, Semans listing, Johansson 37 (illustrated), Supp. 11, Eyo 52.	The Angas tribe of Plateau State and also in Bauchi State, Nigeria.
SALT. Brought by camel caravan from mines in Ethiopia; is also extracted from mineral-rich spring water.		Kierans 8, Sigler 12, 13, Barth 291, 391, 452, Batutta 317, Einzig (1966) 113, Melitz 98, Eyo 40, 55, 69, Opitz 289–293, Wieschhoff 38, Mitton 118, Quiggin 54–56, 82–84 Johansson 55–57, Supp. 15, Hutchinson 254, Guyer 39, 47.	Most tribes in Africa.
SENUFO BOAT ANKLET. This brass anklet is 17 cm x 9 cm (6¾" x 3 5/8") and weighs 600+ g (21.2 oz).		Opitz 278, 281, Mitton 103, Semans list.	The Senufo tribe in Burkina Faso.

Names & Details	Image	Citations	Tribe/Country
SHOKA. Varies in size & wt.: 23–28cm (9–11") length and 113.5–227 g. (4–8 oz.) wt. Made of sheet iron.		Opitz 306, Eyo 33, Kriger 100, 101, Mitton 118, Quiggin 51, 64, 66, 67, Pl. 1, Fig. 7, Pl. 3, Fig. 4.	The Mangbetu tribe in northern DRC. Originally made in Birmingham, England, with inferior materials.
SLAVE. There were domestic slaves and slaves for export to US, Europe, and the Caribbean.		Barth 515, Baikie 387, Bowdich 321, 338, Einzig (1949) 149, Einzig (1966) 111, 114, 131, Guyer 47, 59, Herbert (Red Gold) 132, Hutchinson 112, 113, Melitz 110, Opitz 309, Quiggin 33, 63, Ryder 57, Sigler 12, Sterns 303.	Most of Africa.
SOMBE PENNY (BUJI). A grooved iron rod 22 cm or 23 cm (9 1/8" or 9 ¼") in length with flattened ends; the precursor to the kissi penny.		Blandin 163, Fry 174, Mitton 104, Opitz 92, Semans list.	The Guro, Baule, and Bete tribes of Côte d'Ivoire and also from Liberia.
SPADE HOE. Cast iron, 16 cm x 24 cm (6¼" x 9½"), and has a tang for a wooden handle. Weight is 320 g (11.5 oz).		Baikie 114, 115, Einzig (1966) 110, Mitton 108, Opitz 157, 158, Johansson 38 #3, illustrated, Supp. 11 #36.	The Mambila tribe of Cameroon and Nigeria, the Bamileke of Cameroon, the area of north-central Nigeria and in the Sudan.

Names & Details	Image	Citations	Tribe/Country
STRAW TIN. Was produced by forcing hole into the clay of an old riverbed, pouring in the tin. Length of 25.5 cm (10").		Eyo 55, Johansson 50, 57, Supp. 16, #77, Mitton 119, Opitz 322.	Confined to the tin-producing area on the Jos Plateau in Nigeria.
TAJERE. An iron bar currency with a diamond-shaped swelling at center and long squared ends. 39.5 cm (15¾").		Opitz 332, Baikie 220, Eyo 52, 68, Melitz 98, Joyce 22 Fig. 33, 34, Quiggin 87.	The Batta and Mumuye tribes in Nigeria and also the tribes around the Adamawa Emirate in NE Nigeria.
TOBACCO. Came in many forms: leaf (East Africa), stick (South Africa), coiled (Angola), and also twisted.		Kierans 8, Eyo 69, Kingsley 271, Opitz 352, 353, Mitton 120, Quiggin 103, Wieschhoff 38, 39.	The Kagoro tribe from Zaria, Nigeria, also in Gombe Division, eastern Nigeria, and in Angola, South Africa, and East Africa.
TOGO STONE MONEY (QUARTZ DISC). White quartz disc with diameter 5–6.5 cm (2–2½").		Opitz 273. Reed 31, Quiggin 60, 61, Pl. 3, #3, Semans list, Mitton 119.	The Baoula in Côte d'Ivoire, the Ashanti in Ghana and several tribes in Togo and Sierra Leone.
TROMBASH THROWING KNIFE. Iron, wood, twisted wire. 36.8 cm ht. (14½"), 20.3 cm w. (8").		Quiggin 68, Opitz 357, 358, Joyce 16, Fig. 3, Mitton 120, Ballarini 87–89.	Azande—Sudan & Rep. of Congo; Ubangi, Sankuru, Bushongo, Bakongo, & Mangbetu are all DRC. Bakongo, Angola, Rep. of Congo.

Names & Details	Image	Citations	Tribe/Country
TUKULA (CAMWOOD, NKULU, NGULA). The rotted red-wood is ground down and formed into cakes. Numerous uses.		Kierans 8, Quiggin 80, 81, Opitz 358. Mitton 120, Reed 94.	Bushongo along the Kasai & Sanku-ru Rivers in DRC. Also the Ubangi in the DRC.

Notes

Chapter One

1. A. Hingston Quiggin, *A Survey of Primitive Money* (New York: Taylor & Francis, 1970), 51.
2. *New Oxford American Dictionary*. (Oxford: Oxford University Press, 2006).
3. *American Heritage Dictionary*. (Boston: Houghton Mifflin, 1985).
4. Paul Einzig. *Primitive Money in Its Ethnological, Historical and Economic Aspects* (London: Eyre & Spottiswoode, 1949), 148.
5. H. A. Wieschhoff, "Primitive Money," *University Museum Bulletin* 11 (December 1945): 14.
6. Quiggin, 55.
7. Paul Einzig. *Primitive Money in Its Ethnological, Historical and Economic Aspects*, second edition (Oxford: Pergamon, 1966).
8. Einzig 1949, 146 (second footnote). Each cwt. is multiplied by 112 pounds and the product is divided by 2,000 to convert into tons.

Chapter Two

1. *New Oxford American Dictionary*.
2. Martin Dugard. *Into Africa: The Epic Adventures of Stanley and Livingstone.* (New York: Doubleday, 2003), 135.
3. Quiggin, 6.
4. Anne Hugon. *The Exploration of Africa* (London: Thames & Hudson, 1993), 96.
5. Ibid., 91.
6. Ibid., 54.
7. Ibid., 111.
8. Ibid., 122.
9. Ekpo Eyo, *Nigeria and the Evolution of Money* (Lagos: Central Bank of Nigeria, 1979), 68.
10. Langa Langa, *Up Against It in Nigeria* (New York: E. P. Dutton, 1922), 160, 161.
11. Peter Enahoro. *How to Be a Nigerian.* (Ibadan, Nigeria: Caxton, 1977), 29.

Chapter Three

1. Quiggin, 92.
2. Sonia Bleeker, *The Ibo of Biafra* (New York: William Morrow, 1969), 63–64.
3. Richard Fry. *Bankers in West Africa* (London: Hutchinson Benham, 1976), 108.

4. Mary Douglas, "Raffia Cloth Distribution in the Lele Economy," in *Tribal and Peasant Economies* (Austin, Texas: University of Texas Press, 1967), 107.

5. Ibid., 106.

6. Thomas J. Hutchinson, *Impressions of Western Africa* (London: Frank Kass, 1858), 122–124.

7. Einzig 1949, 31.

8. Enahoro, 18.

9. Eyo, 68.

Chapter Four

1. Ousmanou Ngam, *Armes-Monnaies d'Afrique Noire* (Douala, Cameroon: Avant Propos, n.d.), 4.

2. Quiggin, 92.

3. Mary H. Kingsley, *Travels in West Africa: Congo Francais, Corisco and Cameroons* (London: Macmillan, 1897). Reprinted as *Travels in West Africa*. Mineola, NY: Dover Publications, 2003, 320.

4. Quiggin, 78.

5. Ibid., 75.

6. Charles J. Opitz, *An Ethnographic Study of Traditional Money* (Ocala, FL: First Impressions Printing, 2000), 124.

7. Quiggin, 79.

8. Ibid., 79.

9. Einzig 1949, 151.

10. Eugenia W. Herbert, *Red Gold of Africa* (Madison, WI: University of Wisconsin Press, 1984), 124.

11. Quiggin, 58.

12. Ibid., 59.

13. Ibid., 58.

14. Einzig 1949, 148.

15. Quiggin, 79.

Chapter Five

1. Merrick Posnansky, *The Origins of West African Trade* (Accra, Ghana: Ghana Universities Press, 1971), 4.

2. "Salt Mining," Wikipedia, www.en.wikipedia/saltmininghistory.

3. Edward William Bovill, *The Golden Trade of the Moors* (Princeton: Markus Weiner, 1995), 239.

4. Quiggin, 53.

5. Ibid., 55.

6. Matthew 5:13. *NIV Study Bible* (Grand Rapids, MI: Zondervan, 1985).

7. Ibn Battuta. *Travels in Asia and Africa* (London: Routledge, 1957), 318.

8. Ibid., 319.

9. Bovill, 239.

10. Quiggin, 53.

11. Heinrich Barth, *Travels and Discoveries in North and Central Africa* (London: Frank Kass, 1965), 453.

12. Quiggin, 55.

13. Einzig 1966, 128.

14. Einzig 1949, 156.

15. Sven-Olof Johansson, *Nigerian Currencies: Manillas, Cowries and Others,* 2nd ed. (Norrkoping, Sweden: self-pub., 1967), 47.

16. Ibid., 48.

17. Mary's Legacy: The Mary Slessor Foundation. www.maryslessor.org.legacy.

18. Kingsley, 473.

19. Ibid., 473–475.

20. Sven-Olof Johansson, *Nigerian Primitive Currency Values,* (Beirut: self-pub., 1968), 19. Quote from Sir Alan Burns.

21. Ibid., 19.

Chapter Six

1. Herbert 1984, 33.

2. Colleen E. Kriger, *Pride of Men: Ironworking in Nineteenth-Century West Central Africa* (Portsmouth, NH: Heinemann, 1999), 64–65.

3. Eugenia W. Herbert, *Iron, Gender and Power: Rituals of Transformation in African Societies* (Bloomington: Indiana University Press, 1993), 8.

4. Herbert 1984, 34.

5. Herbert 1993, 38.

Chapter Seven

1. Wikipedia Dictionary, s.v. "noun," 4.

2. Herbert 1984, 210.

3. Ibid., 208. Andrew Battell, late sixteenth century.

4. Ibid., 210. The observation of Pedro de Anhaia upon landing on the Mauritanian coast at the beginning of the sixteenth century.

5. Ibid., 210. A description from Conceicao in 1696.

6. Ibid., 210, 213. An observation of Pieter von Meerhoff, the first European known to visit Namaqualand (present-day Namibia, Botswana, and South Africa).

7. Ibid., 214.

8. Kingsley, 271.

9. One of the items we left the studio with was the lost-wax cast of the bust of the oba pictured on p. 124.

Chapter Eight

1. *New Oxford American Dictionary*.
2. *New Oxford American Dictionary*.
3. Bleeker, 113.
4. Hutchinson, 163.
5. Langa, 224.
6. Ibid., 224.
7. "Tropical Medicine: Cupping," Wikipedia.
    www.tropicalmedecine:cupping.wikipedia.
8. Hutchinson, 70.

Chapter Nine

1. Herbert 1984, 242.
2. Ibid., 244.
3. Ibid., 245.
4. Quiggin, 80.
5. William Balfour Baikie, *Narrative of an Exploring Voyage Up the Rivers Kwo'ra and Benue* (London: Frank Kass, 1966), 304.
6. Herbert 1984, 204.
7. Sir Edward Coke, 1552–1634.
8. Bleeker, 86–89.
9. Mungo Park, *The Travels of Mungo Park* (London, J. M. Dent & Sons, 1923), 15.
10. "Ashanti Empire," Wikipedia. www.en.wikipedia.org/wiki/AshantiEmpire.
11. "Benin Bronzes," Wikipedia. https://en.wikipedia.org/wiki/Benin_Bronzes.
12. Bovill, 81.
13. Edward T. Bowdich, *Mission from Cape Coast Castle to Ashantee* (London: Frank Kass, 1966), 317.
14. Bovill, 81.
15. Bowdich, 254.
16. Ibid., 255.
17. Ibid., 254.
18. Ibid., 260.
19. Ibid., 320–321.
20. Bovill, 81.
21. Herbert 1984, 248.

Chapter Ten

1. Enahoro, 39.
2. Ibid., 41.

3. Ibid., 39.
4. Bleeker, 117.
5. Charles Partridge, *Cross River Natives* (London: Hutchinson, 1905), 177.
6. Baikie, 315.
7. Bowdich, 463.
8. Quiggin, 58.
9. Partridge, 168–169.
10. Kingsley, 484.
11. Ibid., 252.

Chapter Eleven

1. Langa, 33.
2. Quiggin, 78.
3. Ibid., 82.
4. Ibid., 82.
5. Einzig 1949, 19.
6. Herbert 1984, 217.
7. Quiggin, 83.
8 . "Twenty Years of Central Banking in Nigeria, 1959–1979," (Lagos, 1979), 205.

Bibliography

African-American Institute. *The Art of Metal in Africa.* Santa Ana: Bowers Museum, 1983.

Aumann, G. *Primitives Geld.* Coburg, Germany: self-published, n.d.

American Heritage Dictionary. Boston: Houghton Mifflin, 1985.

Baikie, William Balfour. *Narrative of an Exploring Voyage Up the Rivers Kwo'ra and Benue.* London: Frank Kass, 1966.

Ballarini, Roberto. *Black Africa's Traditional Arms.* Milano, Italy: Africo Curio, 1992.

Barth, Heinrich. *Travels and Discoveries in North and Central Africa.* London: Frank Kass, 1965.

Battuta, Ibn. *Travels in Asia and Africa.* London: Rutledge & Kegan Paul, 1957.

Blandin, Andre. "Fer Noir" d'Afrique de l'Ouest. 1992.

Bleeker, Sonia. *The Ibo of Biafra.* New York: William Morrow, 1969.

Bovill, Edward William. *The Golden Trade of the Moors.* Princeton: Markus Wiener, 1995.

Bowdich, Edward T. *Mission from Cape Coast Castle to Ashantee.* Frank Kass, 1966.

Chinmoy, Sri. *Meditations: Food for the Soul.* Sri Chinmoy Centre. 1971.

Curtin, Philip D. editor. *Africa Remembered, Narratives by West Africans from the Era of the Slave Trade.* Madison, WI: University of Wisconsin Press, 1967.

Douglas, Mary. "Raffia Cloth Distribution in the Lele Economy." In *Tribal and Peasant Economies.* Austin, Texas: University of Texas Press, 1967.

Dugard, Martin. *Into Africa: The Epic Adventures of Stanley and Livingstone.* New York: Doubleday, 2003.

Einzig, Paul. *Primitive Money in Its Ethnological, Historical and Economic Aspects.* London: Eyre & Spottiswoode, 1949.

Einzig, Paul. *Primitive Money in Its Ethnological, Historical and Economic Aspects.* Second edition. Oxford: Pergamon, 1966.

Enahoro, Peter. *How to Be a Nigerian.* Ibadan, Nigeria: Caxton Press, 1977.

Eyo, Ekpo. *Nigeria and the Evolution of Money.* Lagos: Central Bank of Nigeria, 1979.

Fage, J. D. *A History of West Africa.* London: Cambridge University Press, 1969.

Forde, Daryll. *Marriage and the Family Among the Yako in South-eastern Nigeria.* London: Percy Lund Humphries, 1951.

Fry, Richard. *Bankers in West Africa.* London: Hutchinson Benham, 1976.

Gebauer, Paul and Clara. *A Guide to Cameroon Art from the Collection of Paul and Clara Gebauer.* Portland, OR: Art Museum, 1968.

Guyer, Jane I., ed. *Money Matters: Instability, Values and Social Payments in the Modern History of West African Communities.* Portsmouth, NH.: Heinemann, 1995.

Herbert, Eugenia W. *Iron, Gender and Power.* Bloomington and Indianapolis: Indiana University Press, 1993.

Herbert, Eugenia W. *Red Gold of Africa.* Madison, WI: University of Wisconsin Press,1984.

Herodotus, trans. Robin Watersford. *The Histories.* 2008.

Herskovits, Melville J. *Economic Anthropology/The Economic Life of Primitive Peoples.* New York: W. W. Norton, 1952.

Hurston, Zora Neale. *Barracoon.* New York: Harper Collins Publishers, 2018.

Hugon, Anne. *The Exploration of Africa.* New York: Harry N. Abrams, 1993.

Hutchinson, Thomas J. *Impressions of Western Africa.* London: Frank Kass, 1858.

Johansson, Sven-Olof. *Nigerian Currencies: Manillas, Cowries and Others, Second Edition.* Norrkoping, Sweden: self-published, 1967.

Johansson, Sven-Olof. *Nigerian Primitive Currency Values.* Beirut: self-published, 1968.

Joyce, Tom. *Life Force at the Anvil: The Blacksmith's Art from Africa.* Asheville, NC: Biltmore Press, 1998.

Kierans, Anthony D. *Primitive Currency.* Braunton, UK: Merlon Books, 1988.

Kingsley, Mary H. *Travels in West Africa: Congo Francais, Corisco and Cameroons.* London: Macmillan, 1897. Reprinted as *Travels in West Africa.* Mineola, NY: Dover Publications, 2003.

Kriger, Colleen E. *Pride of Men: Ironworking in Nineteenth-Century West Central Africa.* Portsmouth, NH: Heinemann, 1999.

Langa, Langa. *Up Against It in Nigeria.* New York: E. P. Dutton, 1922.

Leonard, Robert D. Jr. *Curious Currency: The Story of Money from the Stone Age to the Internet Age.* Atlanta: Whitman Publishing, 2010.

Meek, C. K. *A Sudanese Kingdom, An Ethnographical Study of the Jukun-Speaking Peoples of Nigeria.* London: Kegan Paul, Trench, Trubner. 1931.

Melitz, Jacques. *Primitive and Modern Money: An Interdisciplinary Approach.* Reading: Addison-Wesley, 1974.

Mitton, Charles L. *Ethnic Groups, Artifacts and Traditional Money of Africa Cross Reference Guide.* Denver: self-published, 2005.

New Oxford American Dictionary. Oxford: Oxford University Press, 2006.

Ngam, Ousmanou. *Armes-Monnaies d'Afrique Noire.* Douala, Cameroon: Avant Propos, n.d.

Nitsche, Roland. *Money.* New York: McGraw-Hill, 1970.

NIV Study Bible. Grand Rapids, MI: Zondervan, 1985.

Northern, Tamara. *Royal Art of Cameroon.* Hanover, NH: Dartmouth College, 1973.

Opitz, Charles J. *An Ethnographic Study of Traditional Money.* Ocala, FL: First Impressions Printing, 2000.

Park, Mungo. *The Travels of Mungo Park.* London: J. M. Dent & Sons, 1923.

Partridge, Charles. *Cross River Natives.* London: Hutchinson, 1905.

Posnansky, Merrick. *The Origins of West African Trade.* Accra, Ghana: Ghana Universities Press, 1971.

Quiggin, A. Hingston. *A Survey of Primitive Money,* New York: Taylor & Francis, 1970.

Reader, John. *Africa: A Biography of the Continent.* New York: Alfred A. Knopf. 1997.

Reed, F. Morton. *Odd and Curious.* New York: Sanford J. Durst. 1979.

"Twenty Years of Central Banking in Nigeria: 1959–1979." Lagos: 1979. Research paper.

Ryder, A. F. C. *Benin and the Europeans 1485–1897.* London: Longmans, Green, & Co., 1969.

Schweinfurth, Georg August. *The Heart of Africa.* New York: Harper & Brothers, 1874.

Shaw, Thurstan. *Igbo-Ukwu: An Account of Archaeological Discovery in Eastern Nigeria.* Evanston: Northwestern University Press, 1970.

Sherman, Steven. *Henry Stanley and the European Explorers of Africa.* New York: Chelsea House, 1993.

Sigler, Phares O. *Strange (Odd and Curious) Money of the World.* Silver Springs, MD: self-published, 1954.

Stearns, Robert C. *Ethno-Conchology: A Study of Primitive Money.* Washington D.C.: U.S. Government Printing Office, 1889.

Wiggin, Addison. *The Little Book of the Shrinking Dollar.* Hoboken, NJ: John Wiley. 2012.

Wieschhoff, H. A. "Primitive Money," *University Museum Bulletin* 11 (December 1945).

Zora Neale Hurston National Museum of Fine Arts. *The Art of Money: African Metalwork and Currency.* 2007.

Index

Aberdeen, Scotland 92
aggry beads 29, 182
al-Ghaba 129
Amoo, King 157
Animism 127, 128
Anyun 191
Asantehene 143, 144
Ashanti 125, 143, 144–148, 156, 157
Assin 156
Atlantic slave trade 90–92
Baikie, William Balfour 140
Bale 157, 158
Ballarini, Roberto 122
bamboo bed 142
Bamun bracelet 123
Bangala spearhead 160
Bangles 115, 139, 151
Basanga, Zambia 87
Batakari 190
Baoule anklet 122
beads 28–32, 49, 81, 115, 116, 128,
    140, 167
Benin 29, 63, 64, 118, 124, 145, 155, 182
Benue River 140, 191
Biafran War 50, 128
Bida, Nigeria 73, 73, 191
bikei 65, 186
bitchie 188
black coppers 56
Blandin, André 122
bochie 72
body wrapping 157, 158
boloko 71, 112
Bowdich, T. Edward 156
bowl furnace 100, 102
bracelets 15, 18, 19, 72–74, 109, 112,
    114, 115, 122, 123, 155, 191
brass frog 121
brass or copper rods 49
bride-price 53, 62–72, 76–80, 88, 161

bridewealth 23, 77
Bubu throwing knife 183
Buji 193
Bulgaria 82
burial ceremony 154, 158
burial cloths 158
burial inside the hut 154
Burkina Faso 155, 119, 187, 192
Burns, Sir Alan 97
Burundi 139
Bwaka throwing knife 3, 21, 111, 160,
    183
Calabar rod (okpoho okuk) 49, 72, 183
calico 23, 75, 76, 81, 184
camel 81, 83–87, 117
Cameron, Verney Lovett 35
Cameroon 64, 67, 121, 123, 140, 161,
    185, 188, 189, 193
camwood 118, 154, 195
cannibalism 150, 161
cartridge belt 114
cartridges 27, 114, 142, 184
cassava 154
cattle 16–18, 46, 63, 70, 117, 172, 184
cattle cult 17, 172
Central African Republic 64, 183
Central Bank of Nigeria (CBN) 175, 180
ceremonial money 60
CFA 78
Chad 73
Chambiri 139
chattel slave 89
Cheboo, King 157
cheetem 27–29, 56, 184
coiled arm or leg rings 139, 140
coinage system, steps leading to 180
compass 26, 81, 85
Congo Basin 21, 64, 57, 70, 71, 78, 86,
    139, 190
Coquilhat, Camille-Aimé 117

Coquilhatville, DRC 139
Côte d'Ivoire 146, 147, 186 193, 194
cowrie 1–3, 9–18, 22, 48–51, 57, 77, 81,
    133, 135, 159, 166, 172–174, 185, 191
cupping 131, 133
Dark Continent, The 34
deba 150
Democratic Republic of Congo (DRC)
    75, 48, 88, 182, 183, 185–95
diako 189
double gong 68, 113, 185
dubil 46 113, 47, 185
Duke Town, Nigeria 93
Dundee, Scotland 92
East Africa 63, 68, 117, 183, 185, 194
Edo 145
efufy 191
ehuke 189
Ensuba 185
Equatorial Guinea 118, 161
Ethiopia 48, 87 141, 142, 184, 191, 192
Fan axes 65, 186
Federal Reserve Board 21, 25, 81
fetishes 94, 128, 131, 136
First World War 89
fixed-value currency 59
gifting 52–54
gin 40, 82, 88, 89, 96 117, 186
goat 17, 46, 50, 56, 63, 70, 78, 117, 184
goatskin rug 142
gold 8, 82, 125, 143–150, 156, 157, 179
gold dust 1, 149, 186
gold nugget 146
gold weights (Ashanti) 125
gong 63, 68, 113, 185
goro 187
Gras, Col. Basil 141
Guinea 64, 109, 110, 187
guinea corn 9, 12, 13, 42, 63
guro 193
Haarlem, Netherlands 145
hakuna 191
handa cross 187
Hebron beads 30, 182
hoes 14, 47, 63, 64, 69, 133, 160

hound dogs 150
Ibn Battuta 84, 90
idang 189
idoma 46, 47, 113, 133, 160, 186
Igbo anklet disc 171
Igbo-Ukwu culture 155
ikonga spearhead 20, 66, 186
Industrial Revolution 92
iron bar money 40, 41, 46, 47, 194
iron bell or gong 155
iyayaw 191
Johannesburg, South Africa 78
juju 130
kasuyu 188
Katanga cross 70, 71, 778, 111, 133, 160,
    167, 187
Katanga mine 106
Kenya 17, 31, 14, 172, 183, 184
kilindi 64, 187
king manilla 161
Kingsley, Mary H. 40, 117, 161–163
Kissi penny 9, 17, 18, 47, 64, 65, 67, 109,
    110, 133, 159, 187, 193
kola nuts 9, 37, 63, 117, 118, 119, 155,
    187
Konga leg band 113, 116, 171, 187
Kopo Robert Matsaneng 79
Kriger, Colleen E. 99
Kuba cloth 28, 53, 54, 76, 117, 170, 188
Kukawa market 12, 14, 16
Kumbi, Kingdom of Ghana 129, 145,
    146
kuntu 184
kunu 63
Kwadja double hoe 67, 112, 160, 188
Kwo'ra River 140
Lagos, Nigeria 22, 177
Langtang cloth 184
leg bands 19, 20, 116, 170, 171
Liberia 64, 66, 109,110, 186, 187, 193
liganda 20, 63, 64, 111, 113, 141, 188
Livingstone, David 25, 26, 32, 33, 140,
    184
Lobola 79, 80

Lobola 79, 80
Luba zapozap 188
Luluaberg, Congo Basin 86
M'Kuba 139
machete 26, 78, 96, 142
madiba 53, 76, 78, 188
maître sorcier 106
Cotton, Major Powell 83
Mambila 188, 193
Mandjang 188
Mangbetu throwing knife 110,189
manilla, common 9, 10, 15, 16, 22, 49,
    72, 73, 82, 88, 91, 133, 140, 157, 160,
    172–175, 180, 187, 189
manilla, coiled 189
manilla, king 160, 161
manilla, proto- 192
manilla, queen 160, 161
manilla, wave 73, 74
mapel mahangi 53
Maria Theresa thalers 12, 13, 1, 83, 160,
    166, 168
marks of status 20, 21, 23, 141
marriage hoe 66, 189
master smelter 63, 99, 104–107
mat money 28, 53, 72, 117, 133, 188, 54
matrilineal society 147
Mbole hollow leg band 19, 20, 111, 170,
    189
medicine man 1, 127, 128, 130–135, 154
cloths, men's 158
metallurgical glossary 100–102
Mfumte 188
millefiori beads 30, 182
minkata 112, 139, 140, 189
mitako 190
Mithqal 149, 186
mock shirts 2, 13, 16, 190
Mogadishu, Somalia 69
money changer 47, 49
Munsa, King 151
munseia 190
Munshi axe head 190
Munshi beads 31, 182

narrow hoe 15, 47, 66, 111, 190
native cloth 17, 75
ndoa 188
needle money 47, 48, 91
New York Herald 27, 33
nnganga 106
ngbele see *liganda*
Ngombe throwing knife 67, 160, 191
ngula 195
ngwolo 191
nja 189
nkulu 195
nta 76
Nupe bracelet 74, 74, 112, 141
nyama 107
oba 121, 140, 145, 155
occult 127
Offa, Nigeria 130
ogoja penny 47, 48, 191
okanu 183
Old Calabar, Nigeria 55, 183, 184
Olfert Dapper 145
onganda 191
Onitsha, Nigeria 155, 192
Opitz, Charles J. 121, 122
Osei Tutu 147
ostrich eggshell beads 31, 183
packed-earth bed 142
pagazi 27, 28
palaver 129,148
Park, Mungo 43
proto-manilla see *manilla, proto-*
purr-purr 46, 47, 68, 133, 160, 192
quartz disk 133, 194
Quiggin, A. Hingston 82, 161, 168
raffia cloth 28, 52–54, 76, 78, 113, 117,
    133, 170, 188
Reed, Morton F. 121
riga 154
Roosevelt, Theodore 35
Rotl 10, 17, 18, 135, 159
round hoe 14, 47, 68, 192
Royal Niger Company 168
sacrificial chicken 155

Sahara Desert 36, 81, 84, 85, 153
Sahel 81
salt 16, 22, 81–87, 192
salt block 83, 192
salt crystals 86, 87
Sambanza 140
São Tomé and Príncipe 161
Schweinfurth, Dr. Georg August 150
Semans, Scott 152
Senegal 119, 155, 189
Senufo boat anklet 117, 192
shaft furnace 101, 102, 104
sheep 46, 50, 63, 117, 149, 184
shoka 160, 161, 193
Sierra Leone 64, 109, 110, 118, 133 172, 175, 179, 187, 194
Sigler, Col. Phares O. 121
Sitim 28, 124
slave, as human sacrifice 90
slavery, forms of 89
slavery, historical facts 89
slaves, free will of 89
slaves, rights of 89
Slessor, Mary 92–98, 153
smelter 63, 99, 104–107
Somalia 69
sombe penny 109, 110, 133, 160, 193
sorcery 127
South Sudan 66
spade hoe 15, 47, 68, 193
Spearhead 20, 66, 141, 160, 170, 182
Speke, John Hanning 35
Stanley Pool 158
straw tin 49, 194
Sudan vii, 30, 58, 66, 84, 182, 184, 189, 193, 194
suu 188
symbols of power 137
Taghaza, Mali 84–87
tajere 46, 133, 160, 194
Tanzania 17, 332, 64, 172, 184
Third Anglo-Ashanti War 144
throwing knives 3, 67, 110, 111, 151, 160, 21, 183, 189, 191, 194

Timbuktu, Mali 85
tobacco 40, 117, 118, 194
Togo 63, 68, 133, 149, 185, 186, 194
Togo stone money 133, 194
Topoke 64
trade beads 49, 81, 167, 182
translator 26
trombash throwing knife 110, 111, 189, 194
tukula 117, 118, 195
twins 93–96
twist and knot bochie 72
Ujiji, Tanzania 32, 184
uniformity of money system 167, 168
usitim 28, 184
vek 77, 78
vizier 150
"Western" practices 153
wives, competition between 143
women, prohibitions against 107, 108
women's cloths 158
yakaro 191
yam 37, 155
Zanzibar 25, 32, 35
Zong 188

Photo Credits

Title page: Wave manilla: Stephen J. Zylstra; tajere, courtesy of Hamill Gallery of Tribal Art; Bwaka throwing knife, courtesy of Zamenek-Muenster
Part I, p. 5: Trombash throwing knife: courtesy of Hamill Gallery of Tribal Art
Part II, p. 181: Bamun bracelet: courtesy of Hamill Gallery of Tribal Art

Introduction

Map of Africa: shutterstock.com/Peter Hermes Furian

Chapter One

1. boombox: ©shutterstock.com/stuar
2. Kissi pennies: Stephen J. Zylstra
3. loose cowrie shells and two rotls: Stephen J. Zylstra
4. common manillas: Stephen J. Zylstra
5. Maria Theresa thaler: Stephen J. Zylstra
6. mock shirts, sm./lg.: Stephen J. Zylstra
7. round hoe: Stephen J. Zylstra
8. spade hoe: Stephen J. Zylstra
9. narrow hoe: Stephen J. Zylstra
10. cattle: ©shutterstock.com/ Irmelamela
11. bracelet assortment: Stephen J. Zylstra
12. Mbole hollow leg band: courtesy of Hamill Gallery of Tribal Art
13. Ikonga spearhead: Stephen J. Zylstra
14. Bangala spearhead: courtesy of Hamill Gallery of Tribal Art
15. Mangbetu throwing knife: courtesy of Hamill Gallery of Tribal Art
16. Bwaka throwing knife: courtesy of Zemanek-Muenster

Chapter Two

17. Henry M. Stanley: courtesy of © National Portrait Gallery, London
18. Dr. David Livingston: Thomas Annan/ public domain
19. compass: ©iStock.com/Bet Noire
20. cloth: Stephen J. Zylstra
21. cheetem: courtesy of Rolf Denk
22. aggry beads: Stephen J. Zylstra
23. millefiori beads: courtesy of Unique African Arts
24. Hebron beads: Stephen J. Zylstra
25. Munshi beads: courtesy of coincoin.com

26. ostrich eggshell beads: Stephen J. Zylstra
27. Stanley meets Livingstone: © National Portrait Gallery, London
28. Theodore Roosevelt's Expedition: Theodore Roosevelt, African Game Trails, 1910/ public domain
29. John and Luka with rabbits: Marilyn Zylstra
30. iron bar money: Marilyn Zylstra

Chapter Three

31. market scene: courtesy of Eskil Fredriksson
32. tajere: courtesy of Hamill Gallery of Tribal Art
33. idoma: courtesy of Hamill Gallery of Tribal Art
34. dubi: courtesy of Eucoprimo
35. purr-purr: courtesy of Hamill Gallery of Tribal Art
36. needle money: Marilyn Zylstra
37. ogoja penny: Marilyn Zylstra
38. brass or copper rods: Marilyn Zylstra
39. straw tin: Marilyn Zylstra
40. raffia cloths: courtesy of Hamill Gallery of Tribal Art
41. mancala, the national game of Africa: Marilyn Zylstra

Chapter Four

42. wedding invitation: James P. Zylstra
43. liganda: courtesy of Hamill Gallery of Tribal Art
44. Fan axes: Marilyn Zylstra
45. marriage hoe: courtesy of Hamill Gallery of Tribal Art
46. Kwadja double hoe: Stephen J. Zylstra
47. ngombe throwing knife: Stephen J. Zylstra
48. double gong: courtesy of Hamill Gallery of Tribal Art
49. Somali slave: public domain/Georges Revoil
50. Katanga cross: courtesy of Hamill Gallery of Tribal Art
51. boloko: courtesy of Hamill Gallery of Tribal Art
52. twist and knot bochie: Stephen J. Zylstra
53. wave manilla: Stephen J. Zylstra
54. large Nupe bracelet: Stephen J. Zylstra
55. medium Nupe bracelet: Stephen J. Zylstra
56. 4 Maasai women in calico: courtesy of Anne Menke Gallery/Anne Menke
57. nguni cattle: courtesy of Willow Country Nguni

Chapter Five

58. salt block: Shutterstock.com/Bogdan Florea
59. camel with salt blocks: ©iStock.com/R.Weisswald
60. salt caravan: ©iStock.com/Davor Lovincic
61. salt crystals: courtesy of American Numismatic Society
62. gin bottles: courtesy of Rolf Denk
63. chattel slave (Yoruba) : Shutterstock.com/Armstead and White/Everett Historical
64. Miss Mary Slessor: public domain
65. Nigerian fetish dolls: James P. Zylstra
66. Mary Slessor tombstone: James P. Zylstra

Chapter Six

67. simple bowl furnace: Akgimages.com/Woodcut, 1864, after a drawing by Emil Antoine Bayard
68. more developed bowl furnace: alamy.com/
69. shaft furnace: courtesy of crystalinks.com

Chapter Seven

70. Kissi pennies: courtesy of Hamill Gallery of Tribal Art
71. sombe pennies: Marilyn Zylstra
72. narrow hoe: courtesy of Hamill Gallery of Tribal Art
73. Mbole hollow leg band: courtesy of Hamill Gallery of Tribal Art
74. tajere: courtesy of Hamill Gallery of Tribal Art
75. Mangbetu throwing knife: courtesy of Hamill Gallery of Tribal Art
76. Katanga cross: courtesy of Hamill Gallery of Tribal Art
77. trombash throwing knife: courtesy of Hamill Gallery of Tribal Art
78. Congo leg band: courtesy of Hamill Gallery of Tribal Art
79. boloko: courtesy of Hamill Gallery of Tribal Art
80. Nupe bracelet: courtesy of Hamill Gallery of Tribal Art
81. Kwadja: double hoe courtesy of Hamill Gallery of Tribal Art
82. Senufo boat anklet: courtesy of Hamill Gallery of Tribal Art
83. minkata: courtesy of Hamill Gallery of Tribal Art
84. double gong: courtesy of Hamill Gallery of Tribal Art
85. idoma: courtesy of Hamill Gallery of Tribal Art
86. konga leg band: courtesy of Hamill Gallery of Tribal Art
87. dubil: courtesy of Hamill Gallery of Tribal Art
88. Kuba cloth: courtesy of Hamill Gallery of Tribal Art
89. liganda: courtesy of Hamill Gallery of Tribal Art
90. women/ Konga leg bands: courtesy of Eucoprimo –

91. tobacco: courtesy of leafonly.com
92. tukula: ©shutterstock.com/Marilyn Barbone
93. kola nuts: ©shutterstock.com/Matthias G. Ziegler
94. brass frog: Marilyn Zylstra
95. Baoule anklet: courtesy of Hamill Gallery of Tribal Art
96. Bamun bracelet: courtesy of Hamill Gallery of Tribal Art
97. lost wax casting of oba: Trevor Zylstra

Chapter Eight

98. medicine man: Hans Hillewaert, CC BY-SA 3.0
99. medicine man cupping: courtesy of Welcome Library, London.
100. Togo stone money: courtesy of coincoin.com
101. Almaro Medicine Co.: Stephen J. Zylstra

Chapter Nine

102. minkata on woman: courtesy of Steven Goethals
103. ten men with spears: public domain/michaelbackmanltd.com
104. cartridges: ©IStockphoto/phillipimage
105. Asantehene's old palace: public domain/Mawuna Koutonin http://
www.contramare.net/site/en/100-african-cities
106. Asantehene's new palace: Nikansahrexford/CC BY-SA 3.0
107. gold dust: ©istockimages.com/Beeldbewerking
108. King Munsa, Mangbetu tribe: public domain/Georg Schweinfurth; ImHerzen
von Afrika, 1874

Chapter Ten

109. oba of Benin carving: Marilyn Zylstra
110. Bwaka throwing knife: courtesy of Zamenek-Muenster
111. king/queen manillas: courtesy of coincoin.com
112. shoka: Marilyn Zylstra
113. Miss Mary Kingsley: courtesy of © National Portrait Gallery/ H. Edmunds-
Hull

Chapter Eleven

114. Konga leg band on legs: courtesy of Eucoprimo
115. Igbo brass anklet disc: courtesy of Woolley & Wallis Co. UK
116. WACB one tenth penny 1907: ©shutterstock.com/Yaroslaff
117. British one penny 1912: courtesy of ukcoinage.uk

118. British one-shilling coin 1902: courtesy ukcoinage.uk
119. WACB two shilling note 1918: courtesy of africanbanknotes.com
120. WACB ten shilling note 1916: courtesy of africanbanknotes.com
121. WACB one shilling note 1918: courtesy of africanbanknotes.com
122. gov't. of Nigeria one shilling note 1918: courtesy of africanbanknotes.com
123. WACB ten shilling note 1941: courtesy of africanbanknotes.com
124. WACB twenty shilling note 1934: courtesy of africanbanknotes.com
125. WACB ten shilling note 1953: courtesy of africanbanknotes.com
126. WACB twenty shilling note 1957: courtesy of africanbanknotes.com
127. WACB five pound/100 shilling note 1954: courtesy of africanbanknotes.com

Photo Credits for Data, Image, and Citation Index

Bangala Spearhead courtesy of Hamill Gallery of Tribal Art
Beads, Aggry: Stephen J. Zylstra
Beads, Hebron: Stephen J. Zylstra
Beads, Millefiori: courtesy of Unique African Arts
Beads, Munshi: courtesy of coincoin.com
Beads, Ostrich shell: courtesy of africadirect.com
Boloko (Okanu, Konga): courtesy of Hamill Gallery of Tribal Art
Bubu throwing knife: courtesy of Eucoprimo
Bwaka throwing knife: courtesy of Zemanek-Muenster
Calabar rods, (Okpoho Okuk) : Marilyn Zylstra
Calico (Dotis) : courtesy of fabricwholesaledirect.com
Cartridge: ©istockphoto.com/philipimage
Cattle: courtesy of Willow Country Nguni
Cheetem: Marilyn Zylstra
Cloths, Male, Female, Burial: Stephen J. Zylstra
Congo leg band: courtesy of Hamill Gallery of Tribal Art
Cowrie shells: Stephen J. Zylstra
Double gong: courtesy of Hamill Gallery of Tribal Art
Dubil: courtesy of Hamill Gallery of Tribal Art
Ensuba: courtesy of Hamill Gallery of Tribal Art
Fan, Fang axes: Marilyn Zylstra
Gin currency: courtesy of Dr. Rolf Denk
Gold dust: ©istockphoto.com/Beeldbewerking
Idoma: courtesy of Hamill Gallery of Tribal Art
Ikonga spearhead: Stephen J. Zylstra
Katanga cross: courtesy of Hamill Gallery of Tribal Art
King, queen manillas: courtesy of coincoin.com
Kissi pennies: courtesy of Hamill Gallery of Tribal Art
Kola nuts: ©shutterstock.com/Matthias G. Ziegler

Konga leg band: courtesy of Hamill Gallery of Tribal Art
Kuba cloth: courtesy of Hamill Gallery of Tribal Art
Kwadja double hoe: courtesy of Hamill Gallery of Tribal Art
Liganda: courtesy of Hamill Gallery of Tribal Art
Luba zapozap: Hamill Gallery of Tribal Art
Mandjang: courtesy of Hamill Gallery of Tribal Art
Mangbetu throwing knife: courtesy of Hamill Gallery of Tribal Art
Manillas: James Zylstra
Marriage hoe: courtesy of Hamill Gallery of Tribal Art
Mbole hollow leg band: courtesy of Hamill Gallery of Tribal Art
Minkata: Stephen J. Zylstra
Mitako: Marilyn Zylstra
Mock shirts: Stephen J. Zylstra
Munseia: Marilyn Zylstra
Munshi axehead: Marilyn Zylstra
Narrow hoe: Hamill Gallery of Tribal Art
Needle money: Marilyn Zylstra
Ngombe throwing knife: Hamill Gallery of Tribal Art
Nupe bracelet: Stephen J. Zylstra
Ogoja pennies: Marilyn Zylstra
Onganda Stephen J. Zylstra
Proto manilla: Stephen J. Zylstra
Purr-purr: courtesy of Hamill Gallery of Tribal Art
Round hoe: Stephen J. Zylstra
Salt block: ©shutterstock.com
Senufo boat anklet: courtesy of Hamill Gallery of Tribal Art
Shoka: Marilyn Zylstra
Slaves: Georges Revoil-Public domain
Sombe penny: Marilyn Zylstra
Spade hoe: Stephen J. Zylstra
Straw tin: Marilyn Zylstra
Tajere: courtesy of Hamill Gallery of Tribal Art
Tobacco: courtesy of leafonly.com
Togo stone money: courtesy of coincoin.com
Trombash throwing knife: courtesy of Hamill Gallery of Tribal Art
Tukula: ©shutterstock.com-Marilyn Barbone

Author photo: Lifetouch

About the Author

JAMES ZYLSTRA was born in Grand Rapids, Michigan, in 1932. He taught mathematics in Grand Rapids, Harbor Springs, and Detroit, Michigan. In the early 1970s he spent four years in Nigeria, where he became interested in the objects sold by traders, which he later identified as "primitive money." After retirement, he returned to an old hobby of numismatics, and collected more examples of primitive money. He has exhibited his prize-winning collections in national coin shows, and has given lectures on the subject. He is the author of several articles on numismatics, one of which won second place in the annual literary awards given by the Central States Numismatic Society.

CPSIA information can be obtained
at www.ICGtesting.com
Printed in the USA
FSHW021233230219
55883FS

9 780578 440118